C0-CCO-146

The Binding of Leviathan

The Binding of Leviathan

CONSERVATISM AND THE FUTURE

by

WILLIAM WALDEGRAVE

HAMISH HAMILTON
LONDON

108237

First published in Great Britain 1978
by Hamish Hamilton Ltd
90 Great Russell Street London WC1B 3PT

Copyright © 1978 by William Waldegrave

British Library Cataloguing in Publication Data

Waldegrave, William
 The binding of leviathan.
  1. Conservatism
  I. Title
  320.5'2   JC571

   ISBN 0–241–89866–8

Printed in Great Britain by
Bristol Typesetting Co Ltd,
Barton Manor, St Philips, Bristol

To
V.K.R.

'Socrates's mistake derives from a fallacy in his basic assumption. Certainly unity is necessary to some extent in both a household and a State. But it does not need to be total. There is a point at which increased unity destroys the State, and also a point, short of that, where the State remains, but in a worse condition. It is as if you were to reduce a harmony to unison, or a complex rhythm to a march.'

Aristotle, *Politics*, 1263b, 13-14

Contents

Acknowledgements		ix
Preface		xi

Part I: The Context of Politics

1	The Next Twenty-five Years	3
2	Britain : A Special Problem	9
3	The Growth of Government	12
4	Countervailing Forces to the Growth of Government	25

Part II: Political Possibilities

1	The Political Response	35
2	The Conservative Tradition	41
3	Manipulating the Sovereign State	47
4	The Marxist Second Front	51
5	Liberalism	59
6	A Conservative-Liberal Common Cause : The Separation of Powers	73

Part III: Conservatism, Community and The Future

1	Introduction	89
2	The need for Conservative Community	90
3	Community and the Future	97
4	Community and Nation	101
5	The Decline of Community	108
6	Community and Corporate State	119
7	From Philosophy to Action	124

Part IV: Policy

1	A Conservative Approach to Incomes Policy	129
2	Industrial and Urban Dereliction : A Conservative Approach	134

Part V: Conclusion

	The Conservative Tradition	147
Bibliography		151
Index		159

108237

108534

Acknowledgements

Many friends have helped and encouraged me to produce this essay. John Roberts, Jim Urmson and Sam Beer taught me philosophy and political theory in the first place. Sir Ian Gilmour, Victoria Rothschild and Sir Dick White made me start writing; Sam Brittan, Sir Keith Joseph, Jim Urmson and Sir Arnold Weinstock read and improved a very inadequate first version of part of the argument; Gillon Aitken, Robin Butler, Lord Rothschild, Victoria Rothschild, Roger Scruton, Jim Urmson and Sir Dick White read the full draft and made many useful improvements and suggestions, as did Christopher Sinclair-Stevenson of Hamish Hamilton, without whose practical support I would never have completed the book. Karen Leigh and Gay Lewis struggled heroically with my hand-writing. My employer, the General Electric Company Ltd., was generous in allowing me leave to do some research; my college, All Souls, in providing the facilities for me to do it in comfort; and the London Library in letting me keep several vital books much longer than their rules allow. My mother showed me, by her own historical work, that it was possible to put pen to paper; and my wife Caroline demonstrated incredible forbearance by putting up with a first draft while we were courting, a second while we were on honeymoon and a third while we were moving house without, as would have been understandable, suing for divorce before the proofs arrived. I am grateful to all these, and others too; but they would not thank me if I tried to claim that they were responsible for what follows.

All Souls College, Oxford
December, 1977.

A*

Preface

The object of this book is not to attempt to write a long Manifesto for the Conservative Party, nor to write a history of the Conservative tradition. The former would be pointless since the Party is successfully generating policy as it goes about its electoral business, and the latter would take me into a competition with Lord Blake and Sir Ian Gilmour[1] which I should not win.

What I shall try to argue is that Conservatism *means* something, that the Conservative[2] tradition still exists—separate and opposed to Liberalism and Socialism in their various forms, though not quite the same sort of creature as they—and that it offers a solid base for dealing with Britain's problems in the next decades. Both the guesswork about the future and the specific policies advocated here and there in the book are included, literally, for the sake of argument, since a political theory is not useful if it appears to bear no relation to the future, and if practical policies cannot be derived from it.

[1] Lord Blake's 1968 Ford Lectures, *The Conservative Party from Peel to Churchill* (Eyre and Spottiswoode, London 1970) is an essential handbook on the history of the Conservative Party. Sir Ian's two books, *The Body Politic* (Hutchinson, London 1969), and *Inside Right: a Study of Conservatism* (Hutchinson 1977) are not only stimulating works of practical, historical, and philosophical politics but are also thick with apt references and quotations.

[2] There is an intractable problem about upper and lower case Conservatives and Liberals. As will emerge, I do not think that the present Liberal Party has much to do with Liberalism in the only sense of that word which has any meaning. Equally there are genuine Conservatives in other parties than the Conservative. In America the situation is worse: 'Liberal' there has come to mean anything on the left. I hope it will be clear that when I use the word 'Liberal' I do not mean a member of the British Liberal Party (or the Australian, for that matter) nor the likes of Professor J. K. Galbraith, who is a Socialist. Semantic problems are bound to arise when parties and professors use fine old words so indiscriminately, for their own purposes.

But it is the central argument—that there is a distinctive Conservative tradition representing a point of view about the relationship between man and the organisations within which he lives and works (here called communities) and between those communities and the State—which is essential to the book.

When practical men and women of affairs gather round some valuable piece of furniture—the coffin-shaped table of the Cabinet room, the great square version in that grandest of Cabinet Office Committee rooms, King Charles's Old Treasury, or the humbler oblong of the Leader of the Opposition's room around which Shadow Cabinets meet—they have various general ideas in mind against which to judge alternative policies.

They have personal considerations, of career, of a lack of understanding of one option, or public commitment to another. They have motives derived from the positions in the constitutional apparatus in which they find themselves : the seeking or retention of electoral support, for example, or the carrying on in orderly fashion of the Queen's government.

The interplay of these two classes of considerations alone would—and in many cases does—provide enough argument to go on with. But there is also a third category—the category of political and social beliefs which, transformed or not into practical objectives, have brought those particular people into public life and maintained them in it when the first spurious glamour of public recognition has long since lost its interest. These underlying ideas—consciously formulated as ideology, or unconsciously trusted as instinct—inform both personal ambitions, by giving promise of more lasting influence than the ephemeral rewards offered by two or three years in a Ministry, and also the participants' views of their constitutional role : for any judgement of what people want, or of what *is* proper order in affairs implies a background of political theory against which both can be assessed.

These underlying ideas are the common currency of a political culture at any time. They overlap between parties and shift between parties over time, though—as this book will argue—there remains a relatively stable divide between those on both sides who seek an over-arching, all-explaining theory, and those who do not. At the moment the coinage of this currency would include (in addition to the small change derived from the personal and institutional motivation mentioned above):

Does this policy tend to produce economic growth?

Does this policy tend to lessen inflation?

Does this policy tend to lessen material differences in possessions between citizens?

Does this policy tend to provide more employment?

Does this policy tend to increase the individual liberty of the citizen?

Does this policy weaken or strengthen Britain in her relations with other nations?

Does this policy bring up to date antique practices?

Does this policy preserve valued survivals?

Does this policy advance/retard the position of category x of our citizens whom we regard as being specially important?

The list can be expanded, though not indefinitely: a good list would describe the topics of political argument of an era.

The purpose of this book is to try to restore to prominence one consideration to which, I believe, it is the distinctive contribution of the Conservative tradition to assign its proper value, namely:

Does this policy tend to advance the chance of the citizen to live, work and play in the kind of communities which are necessary to civilised life?

The book will attempt to explain what is meant by community—a word not much increased in usefulness by its widespread use in recent political rhetoric—and why its growth and preservation needs to rank higher amongst our priorities in the light of problems we are likely to face in the next decades. In fact, it will be argued that a proper regard for community will be found to lead indirectly to success with several other objectives, objectives the direct pursuit of which may have perverse results.

In so doing, the book argues that the future sees a role of increasing importance and relevance for the Conservative tradition as the tradition of community, and increasing success for the party which, though it cannot claim to monopolise the support of Conservatives, is the main guardian of that tradition.

PART I

The Context of Politics

CHAPTER ONE

The Next Twenty-five Years

1. *In Defence of Futurology*

What are likely to be the dominant problems of the next quarter century? It is the politician's job to try to act the role of masthead look-out on the democratic ship of state. He may find that a vote by those in the taffrail bar declines to allow the possiblity of the existence of the rocks he sees ahead, or, in other moods, of the navigable channel he sees through them; nonetheless, he must shout, in the hope that someone will listen. He must not be put off by the fact that sometimes he will see mirages; nor by the fact that, if he guides the ship safely, the general opinion is likely to be that his job is too easy, if not unnecessary, and his pay should be suitably diminished forthwith.

The danger is, of course, that the literally unpredictable so often upsets even the best assessment of the predictable. But this is no reason to give up the enterprise. The unpredictable, after all, by its nature, may not in fact occur; and though a sensible philosophy of politics will be one which is not destroyed too easily by the unexpected, no philosophy will attract much rational support if it does not make some kind of case for saying that it is a philosophy which is going to be of more than ephemeral interest. This study argues that the philosophy embodied in the Conservative tradition is likely to increase in usefulness in the next period of British and European history, rather than diminish, as is persuasively argued by some of its opponents.

2. *A World of Shortages*

What then of the future? Some trends may surely be safely extrapolated. We are entering the era of shortages. The population of the world continues to increase by perhaps one hundred million people a year, or nearly twice the total population of the United Kingdom; our own population and that of most other advanced countries may be, or shortly be, stable, but in world-wide terms the effects of this will be far outweighed by the still increasing population of the less industrialised world.[1] Thus, though there is much productive capacity to take up yet, the scarcity of food, land, water, clothing and energy for an expanding world population will continue to mean that the prices of these and other essential goods will rise. It is hoped that such price rises will be transitional: stimulating new supplies and new technologies, and discouraging wasteful demand. In the meantime, they will still be real. Such scarcities of essentials, however, will have perverse effects of surplus and over-production in the short term of industrial goods in industrial countries: it takes much longer for a country to reorganise itself away from making petrol-engined motor cars which cannot be used in such numbers since the price of the petrol to drive them has risen as a result of shortage, than it does for the shortage of crude oil to become apparent. But in the longer term, the effect of shortage will be to draw attention to the unfair distribution of resources between populations of different sizes, and in particular, the unfair distribution of land; second, it will force the over-populated countries to trade the only resource they have—cheap labour.

3. *The Unfair Distribution of Land*

Strains on national boundaries are likely to increase as population tries to equalise itself round the world; above all, North America and to a lesser extent Western Europe, the former a lightly populated temperate region, and the latter capable of supporting many millions in addition to its likely numbers, will face unremitting pressure for immigration from over-populated nations. This will take the form of individual attempts to avoid legal limits where these are erected and, increasingly, of government-to-government pressure to dismantle or relax such limits once erected. Once, when population roughly coincided with

[1] The Secretary General of the United Nations predicted as his 'Medium Variant' a world population of 6.1 billion in the year 2000 in his Note of November 1969. See also Herman Kahn, William Brown and Leon Martel: *The Next 200 Years* (London 1977), Chapter 1.

military strength (though the big battalions could never be sure that they would not run up against a bottle-neck like the pass of Thermopylae, plugged by a handful of Spartans ignorant of the necessities of history) this dilemma would have been resolved by forcible migration and we might have expected to see Chinese on the plains of the American North-West. Modern weaponry seems to preclude such a solution now; so the present distribution of land, deriving from Europe's maritime ascendancy in the last four centuries, settled before the modern growth of world-wide population, and more capable of maintenance by military superiority than were such distributions in the past, is likely to cause increasing tensions, insoluble by presently existing institutions. What is more, since the rate of increase of population seems to depend on the extent of national development, and not on *Lebensraum* itself, the gap will not be filled by Americans populating their continent, or Asians depopulating theirs.

Movement of people, legal or illegal, will therefore increase as far as it can. Beyond that, areas of the world where no nuclear weaponry intimidates the invader may expect to see an increase in traditional warfare aimed at territorial aggrandisement. In the nature of things, it is also likely that someone will try it, even where threat of nuclear retaliation does exist. The ensuing radiation contamination will further deplete the supply of useful land.

4. *Shifting Industry*

Surplus population is much more conducive to an increased industrial production, since it provides cheap labour, than to efficient agriculture, where it usually implies a social organisation, like peasant smallholding or the self-supporting communal farm, which militates against the large fields and heavy capitalisation of modern agriculture. Thus we should expect to see a continued trend, formidable in its implications, towards a North America, an Australasia and a Europe rich in food, and an India, a Russia, a China, an Africa, and, perhaps, a South America paying for their food with industrial goods. Hermann Kahn, in his Hudson Institute study The *Next 200 Years*,[2] thinks that the surplus populations will be fed by being brought to the old industrialised countries as temporary workers, and then returned home. But

[2] Op. cit.

racial tensions in the industrial centres will surely stop this. The work will go to the workers. The trend is already noticeable : but electronic goods in South-East Asia, textiles in India, cars in Spain and Mexico, ships (for a time) in Japan, are probably only the forerunners of computers in China, telephone equipment in Brazil and engineering components in Indonesia. Only high tariff walls will prevent old established Western industries succumbing to the weight of the Third World's advantage in cheap labour, in the scale of their developing home markets— and also, perhaps, in the ruthlessness with which mass societies alien to the Liberal tradition will organise and discipline their cheap labour and exclude non-essential imports. The omens of China and Japan are already there.

The counters with which the West will be able to bargain, besides tariffs and food, will be its skills : as the history of Soviet technology has shown, it is exceedingly hard to compete with the scientific prowess of the West, now deeply embedded in the culture for some hundreds of years, and supported by a complex web of social and governmental incentives. You cannot invent the scientific traditions of Cambridge or Heidelberg Universities —though you may succeed in transplanting them and refertilising them in California. You can, however, find the dexterous workers to make the computers designed by California or Cambridge in Singapore or Korea.

Thus a West of agricultural wealth, of under-populated territory, of high technology (some of it devoted to the defence of its territory), and of scientific and other skills, will face the countries of big population, scarce territory and food, mass production, and lesser skills. The two could be economically complementary : though it is unlikely that the poorer countries would accept their role, and, even if they did, serious dangers to the West would follow the immense strides of readjustment away from its own industrial traditions which such a world would imply, and from the possibility that some highly-populated country would accept the military risks inherent in an attempt at major territorial aggrandisement. But what of the East?

5. *Can the Russian Empire Survive?*

So far, we have suggested that underlying forces, outside their immediate control, would tend to push Britain and the West in the following directions. Abroad, over-population and scarcity of essentials will increase tension between areas with food and with space and areas without food and without space. Large scale labour-intensive manufacturing industry will move to areas of high population, low pay, and authoritarian government. The Western world and its world-wide outposts, such as Australia, will maintain a balance partly based on military strength derived from high technology, which will prevent the actual shifts in population which might otherwise equalise the density of population; partly on its control of most of the world's agricultural surplus; and partly on its scientific and technological traditions, which will not quickly be matched by the populous countries of China, the Indian subcontinent, Africa and South America.

What of the last remaining Victorian Empire, that of Russia? The continuance of an Empire of far eastern territories acquired in the 1840's (Vladivostock was founded in 1860, by which time Britain had been ruling India for nearly a century) and completed by the conquest of European territory finally subdued only in the last thirty years, is a strange anomaly. It has maintained itself thus far on the basis of a ruthless and efficient imperial ideology which, like all such, claims to bring the word of objective truth to those who might otherwise be without it, and thereby to benefit the benighted even if they do not appreciate it. Thus is justified the coercion necessary for empire. Together with the ideology goes an unusually tough centralised bureaucratic and military machine.

The weaknesses of this Empire are the usual ones. It is difficult to make an ideology which is simple enough to be useful for running the imperial bureaucracy down to its lowest levels, also interesting enough to maintain the allegiance of the outstanding men of action or the subtle thinkers; we may expect to see Leninism increasingly breed its own problems in terms of the dissidence of the ablest Russians. It is difficult to combine the centralised political force necessary for imperial rule with efficient production, which in a large territory must rely on devolved decisions: and the inefficiency of Soviet industry, and above all Soviet agriculture, provides the probable source of future popular discontents on which the increasing number of dissidents may be able to seize. What is more, these inefficiencies in production make the Soviet Union more, not less, dependent on Western food and Western technology (for example to extract its resources of oil and gas) the further it moves from 1917.

6. *The Dangers of Soviet Disintegration.*

Thus Russia adds to the dangers of the world because it poses an antique problem, long since left behind by the Europeans: namely, how to shed an empire. The danger stems from the fact that Russia does not yet see that that is her problem. She will not in the foreseeable future relinquish her sway voluntarily, and may cause increasing problems in her decline. Her ideology cannot retreat and survive: expansionism is inherent in its belief that it has hold of the final truth. The East German, Czechoslovakian and Hungarian uprisings are likely to be the pattern of the future; without an ideology of release for the subject peoples, Russia will once again (as she did at the end of the nineteenth century) collapse from the centre. Once again she will put her neighbours at risk—and particularly her eastern neighbours who cannot but be concerned with what happens as Russia's eastern empire disintegrates. She is not likely to play a decisive role in the future in the sense of influencing the new issues, since she is somewhat set aside from them; but, like some great dinosaur released by a political Professor Challenger into the modern world, she may kill a lot of us before she succumbs to the alien environment.

CHAPTER TWO

Britain: A Special Problem

1. The Trade Imbalance

For Britain the prognosis is disturbing. As a separate national entity, we are massive importers of food, and are almost as densely populated as some of the Asian countries. We are heavily dependent on exporting manufactured products—many of them of the very type whose production is most likely to shift to areas of cheap and disciplined labour, such as cars. We have failed in the three high technology fields on which we have expended the greatest resources of scientific skill and scarce money since the war: aircraft, nuclear power, and computers. In all three of these, home industries are only maintained by a high level of covert or open protection, and in none of them have we established an international trade to replace our lost dominance in ships, textiles and heavy machinery. If the Comet had not crashed; if the Advanced Gas-Cooled Reactor had worked on time; if the British Computer Industry had followed a different strategy. . . . There are many excuses, and many still considerable achievements; but at the end of the day we have failed as traders in high technology, with the one exception—ironic in view of the relatively pacific tendency of our politics since the war—of weapons.

2. Britain: New Investment or New Poverty?

Thus Britain is likely to present one of the most difficult problems in the Western world. A large importer of increasingly scarce food; dependent on many manufacturing industries which may move elsewhere; a failure so far, compared with our competitors, as traders in high technology; densely populated. Twenty years as an oil exporter will allow us, for twenty years, to consume more of the production of other nations in exchange for oil as payment; but it seems inescapable that severe dislocation is threatened by the trends which face us—dislocation which some others, such as Italy and perhaps Japan, will face too, but with which others, such as America, Canada, France and Germany will, for differing reasons, be better equipped to deal.

We will have some difficult choices to make. To retain our share of older manufacturing industries we can only compete with foreign cheap labour by taking very large strides towards labour-saving investment, or by falling back ourselves to the position of a cheap-labour country. The former meets resistance from those who would lose at once jobs which they might otherwise retain rather longer, and who see little prospect of similar numbers of new jobs growing in new industries. It is, in addition, difficult to see where the capital would come from for investment on this scale. Industries are not allowed, by government responding to social pressure, to create the necessary surpluses, while government itself is a notoriously inefficient investor in industry for reasons more to do with the inevitable differences between political and industrial decisions and decision-makers than with ideological villainy. Governments will doubtless try using the oil revenues; this means the oil revenues will be of less value than they might otherwise have been. We would do better to buy efficient firms abroad than to waste money letting Whitehall try to create them here.

The course we are following at present, as inflation and depreciation of our currency steadily depresses the real living standards —and the real cost—of workers in Britain relative to other Western nations is to become a nation of cheap workers. But the strains and resentment this process causes result in such social and political chaos that we are unlikely to be left in a position to benefit from it : rather, the danger is of resentment spilling over and damaging political institutions and social order. If this happened, it would make us a relatively less attractive source of cheap labour to the international investor than others.

3. Britain: The Politics of Declining Industries

Severe problems can be expected to derive from the interaction between an external industrial and trading world changing significantly in ways not helpful to us, and an industrial establishment at home which gives great power to the representatives of what now exists to resist change. The bigger and older an industry—take mining, shipbuilding, or car-manufacture—the more powerful it is politically compared to newer, often less unionised or less highly labour-intensive industries. In the nature of things, leaders of these declining industries promise their constituents to use their power to preserve the *status quo*, and not to dissolve their own power base. And use it they do. One of the effects of this attempt to maintain a lost world is the growth of the power of the state. The next chapter examines the connection between industrial decline and illiberal politics .

CHAPTER THREE

The Growth of Government

1. *Lobbies and Democracy.*

The political effect of the attempt to maintain what exists in the face of hostile reality goes some way towards explaining the tendency in Britain for a faster growth of government than elsewhere : it also largely explains such growth in other countries. The political strength of the elderly, labour-intensive industries produces insistent pressure for more and more government protection, usually ending in nationalisation and demands for direct and open-ended subsidy. Thus such industries, whether formally nationalised or not, are built into the apparatus of the state, greatly increasing its scope. Such subsidy, which amounts to compulsory diversion of the money they generate away from potentially growing industries towards those in decline, makes even less likely the new investment which might possibly produce some new jobs, and perpetuates the process. Thus declining industries are built into government and have a louder voice there than industries on which, in fact, the future rests.

Other powerful forces are at work to produce a spread in government activity too.

First, the growth of pressure-group politics, in which different groups compete for support from government funds, has meant a new generation of skilful media-manipulators. Examples are Trades Unions, charities like Shelter or the Child Poverty Action Group, the Arts Lobby, the BMA, industrial lobbies like the Aircraft Industry. They have little in common except their common demand for government action and expenditure. Such lobbies, worthy in their intentions, mesh disastrously, via the gearing of lobby-susceptible media, with a House of Commons always much more effectively interested in the scandal of the individual case or category of need, than in warning of the dangers which might

ensue from meeting it. The former is, after all, an easier job:
the member who cries 'more money for Bristol' will get a much
kinder hearing in his local papers than the one who argues for less
government money in Bristol, even if everywhere else is to suffer
too, and even if Bristol will share the general benefit of lower
inflation. As has often been said representative democracy can
work rather like a competitive market itself, with bid and counter
bid increasingly in direct money terms, for the voters' support.[1]
Unfortunately, it is a market with no equilibrium. The bidding
process, highly inflationary itself, since it inevitably works to
create expectations of provision unrelated to supply, further
enhances the attraction of a set of economic and political beliefs
which state that the way to reconcile promises with delivery is
by a commitment to economic growth. We look at these beliefs
in the next paragraph.

2. *Economic Growthmanship.*

Thus the democratic system, as it has been recently worked,
seeks out those economists who offer a theory of growth which
will make respectable a process whereby politicians promise ever
larger slices of the national cake to those whose support they
seek. Democratic Socialists, Anthony Crosland, for example in
his *The Future of Socialism*[2] could avoid the bitterness of the
class war—and win the middle class support they needed for
victory—by arguing that state intervention could produce such
gains in production that the workers would attain their just
deserts without revolution. Conservatives could argue to the
identical conclusion, for example in the Conservative Manifesto
of 1970—and win the working class support they needed for
victory—from the opposite starting point. Redistribution went
down the agenda, lessening political bitterness; increase of production went to the top; the political world appeared briefly to
have achieved a state where ideology was dead.

The economic theory which appeared to offer this resolution
was of course associated with the followers of Keynes, who

[1] Originally by Joseph Schumpeter, in *Capitalism, Socialism, and Democracy* (2nd edition, London 1947); more recently by Sam Brittan in his
Capitalism and the Permissive Society (London 1973).
[2] London, 1956.

appeared to be saying that, with sufficiently careful management of demand, continuous growth would be extracted from the economy at the acceptable cost of a small 'pump priming' rate of inflation. Such demand management, combined with various forms of direct intervention on the 'supply side' (in the jargon of the day)—in terms of investment in 'bottle neck' industries, or to clear restrictive practices—would steadily increase the size of the 'national cake'. In this way, the edge could be taken off the battle between competing groups, whether in terms of satisfying electoral promises, or blunting class war.

Sadly, what Keynes himself was arguing was merely the more modest—and undoubtedly true—proposition that when there are many idle resources of men and machines in a country, and assuming that an increase in money supply can be directed in such a way that it will increase demand for the potential products of these men and machines, then in those circumstances an increase in the money supply need not be a source of real inflation. He did not claim that he had found the trick of producing a steady and predictable increase in production once supply and demand had been matched—once the slack had been taken up and the underlying capacity of the country had been reached. What is more, not only did Keynes not claim to have discovered a formula for ensuring a steady growth of the underlying productive capacity, but it is one of the few indubitable truths of economics that no one knows such a formula; or rather, every economist knows it, and no two agree as to what it is. Partly, this may be because economics is not an experimental science: it can never isolate causes and effects with sufficient certainty to predict their sequence in the future; partly, the difficulty derives from the fact that far more social variables are involved in the question whether a society is to produce and consume steadily more, than those which economics attempts to measure. Whatever the reasons, the fact remains, that any economist who says to a politician that he can recommend policy-action which will produce more than short-term growth when resources are unused is making an unjustifiable claim; any politician who bases his political philosophy on the implementation of such a claim has built his house upon sand.

In the past growthmanship has resulted in a massive extension of government. First, when demand was to be increased, government expenditure was regularly used as one way of increasing it, and Departments relaxed their controls and pushed forward new programmes which were not dismantled when the boom was followed by recession. Second, direct intervention in industry, aimed at clearing bottlenecks which were all, it was thought, that stood in the way of a higher growth rate, spawned systematic intervention by government in industry (to add to its support for declining industries). The process started with the Conservative invention of the National Economic Development Council in 1961 and reached its most developed form (so far) in the Labour Government's Industrial Strategy launched in 1975.

We are not finished with this process yet. Failure is not seen by the practitioners of this approach as casting doubts on its correctness; indeed, rather the opposite: failure redoubles the enthusiasm. As Harold Macmillan wrote in his seminal *Middle Way* in 1938—a book which is one of the manifestoes of this approach to demand and to industry: 'The weakness of partial planning seems to me to arise from the incomplete and limited application of the principles of planning. The lesson of these errors, which I regard as errors of limitation, is not that we should retreat. On the contrary, we must advance, more rapidly and still further, upon the road of conscious regulation.'[3]

This philosophy—what might be called the philosophy of the Charge of the Economic Light Brigade—will carry us yet further towards the expansion of government, before it dies.

3. *The End of Growthmanship and the Death of Social Democracy.*

In the next decade we will see the crumbling of the political philosophies based on growth theory. We may, therefore, expect to see a return to political argument based on rival solutions to newly desperate questions about the distribution of a cake the growth of which will be increasingly recognised to be beyond the influence of politicians. Thus we are likely to see the death of social democracy, as it is understood in Britain, on the one hand

[3] Harold Macmillan, *The Middle Way* (London 1938), p. 11.

and Conservative growthmanship on the other, not as a result
of the weakness or strength of individual representatives of those
creeds, but as the result of the passing of the era of confident
social science which enabled both to confine political discussion
largely to arguments about techniques of increasing wealth. Mr
Jenkins and Mr Maudling are not the victims of political putsches
in their own parties; what has failed is not their political skills,
but the theories exposition of which gave them their importance.
The rise of Sir Keith Joseph and Mr Anthony Wedgwood
Benn is not the result of their superior capacities, but of the
fact that they represent theories other than those of growthmanship.

4. *Relative Deprivation*

W. G. Runciman[4] and Fred Hirsch[5] offer another reason why
growth will fall from its central place in the political pantheon.
Not only can we not be sure how to achieve it, but even if we
could, it would not necessarily turn the trick of avoiding conflict
in society. The reason for this is that people perceive their positions relatively to others : even if, over time, I become better off,
I am not much pleased by this if I am not much better off
relative to others. Deprivation, in Runciman's phrase, is relative;
what is more, says Hirsch, the very objectives of growth, traditionally defined, are those benefits possessed by the few, which,
by definition lose their attraction, or actually disappear, when
the many get their hands on them, like country solitude.

Both writers make these insights the basis for an argument for
the further extension of government action : Runciman to equalise wealth compulsorily; Hirsch, more subtly, following a point
of Keynes', to make the competition for unattainable goods less
keen by lowering the stakes. Once the game is less fierce, because
the prizes less interesting, the way is open to encouraging a
morality of co-operation necessary, he argues, since only by collective action can individuals achieve a solution they would
themselves prefer.

[4] W. G. Runciman, *Relative Deprivation and Social Justice* (Penguin, London 1972).
[5] Fred Hirsch, *Social Limits to Growth* (Routledge and Kegan Paul, London 1977).

Thus powerful justifications are still being adduced from the developing nature of society for further expansion of government. They will reinforce already existing trends derived, as we have argued, from the way in which our industrial and political establishments do business with one another, and from the way in which Parliamentary elections are fought.[6]

5. A Return to the Land?

The external issues of living space, food and immigration will also affect us at home. Britain will have to look seriously to reversing the trend of capital and labour away from her agriculture; as a temperate country which, though highly populated, is also (unlike, say, Japan) very unevenly populated, our ability to reduce dramatically our dependence on imported food will be a crucial asset. Dispersal from cities, of non-agricultural population and industry, will need to be reversed both by relative wage levels and by planning. Green-field sites should not now be available for development; it is scandalous that they are; and they will shortly not be.[7] It is probable that the agricultural economy must become, in the long term, much richer in terms both of profits and wages. This will mean that the drift away from political interest in the production of food to its cheap consumption will be reversed. More labour will be needed on the land as more marginal land again becomes economic, and more intensive methods increasingly come to mean small production of multifarious foods in all sorts of pockets of now unused land, as well as efficient use of large units. The cumbersome and out-dated machinery of the Common Agricultural Policy is unlikely in its present form to be equal to the agricultural challenge

[6] A further interesting conclusion is reached by Wilenski, to the effect that the growth of state welfare (a large section of total state activity) correlates much more closely with economic development than with adherence to different political philosophies in the sixty-four countries he analysed. H. L. Wilensky: *The Welfare State and Equality* (University of California, 1975).

[7] The Centre for Agricultural Strategy at the University of Reading, chaired by Lord Rothschild, produced a report in 1976, *Land for Agriculture* (Reading 1976), which showed that Britain has more than enough land in urban derelict and semi-derelict sites for any conceivable housing needs in the next twenty-five years.

ahead, though its *intention*, of raising European food production, will be vindicated.

6. *Illegal Immigrants.*

Illegal immigration will be the crime of the future faced by those countries with large enough present communities to act as a screen for the absorption of new arrivals. A whole list of subsidiary crime, operated by the illegal carriers on the basis of blackmail of those they have brought, will parallel the same phenomenon at the turn of the century in the United States. It will be exceedingly difficult to stop without illiberal controls or even with them, and without the exacerbation of race relations in the host country and internationally. Such is the price the sovereign nation state will have to pay for the erection of inflexible barriers against the movement of peoples.

7. *Demands on the Political System.*

These conflicts are likely to be reflected by a steady growth in demands for the protection of declining industries. This is likely to be the first concern of traditional Trades Unions and of many company managements as they try to use their weight to maintain the *status quo.* Then, food prices rising steadily in the long term will transfer resources away from urban industrial centres declining from their nineteenth century heyday to the agricultural countryside; there will be tremendous problems of urban decline in the big cities which have little connection with their agricultural hinterlands. Small country towns should prosper. Extremist political parties in the big cities would be likely beneficiaries of these problems, and it is hard to see how these parties will avoid a racial basis—since many of those left in the most difficult circumstances of unemployment and decayed housing will be black. Racial solidarity by blacks will be likely to produce equal and opposite political reaction. The tension of the racial situation is likely to be further inflamed by the steady pressure of illegal immigration and the measures necessary to control it.

So, both in the declining manufacturing sector and in the derelict cities, extremist politics are likely to flourish: on the left the demands will be for protection, rationing and controls to protect uncompetitive industries, and for confiscation of the wealth generated in agriculture and associated industries, and in the export of high technology and other skills. On the right, the programme will be much the same, with a racialist flavour and a probable steady growth in demands for the repatriation of immigrants.

8. A New Trade Unionism?

The relative ineffectiveness of the whipped House of Commons as a defender of the non-organised citizens will produce in the short term a stampede into membership of available groups. This will have marked and paradoxical effects on the Trades Union movement. The traditional Trades Union movement, based in the public sector and in large manufacturing industry[8] and increasingly protectionist and industrially reactionary, will find itself declining in numbers—though not, probably, for some time in the weight given to its leaders in the councils of the TUC and the Labour Party. The new Trades Unionists—white collar workers in technical and science based industries, managers, administrative employees of government, agricultural workers, owners and operators of small businesses, the self-employed, the police and, perhaps, the armed forces—are likely to owe little to the traditions of the older Trades Union movement. Memories of the match-girls' battles or the General Strike or the 1974 coal miners' disputes are unlikely to evoke support from new groups the origins of whose organisation lie not in fear of over-mighty employers, but in fear of over-mighty manual workers' unions. At present, something less than half the working population is unionised, predominantly those in old labour intensive industries and large manufacturing operations. These declining sectors will form the basis of power for an ageing traditional unionism, with which the new groups will have few interests in common. They will possess a different demonology, different

[8] The Bullock Report shows that out of 11.8 million Trade Union members in Britain in 1974, 9.8 million or 83% worked either in the public sector or in firms employing more than 2,000 people. Report of the Commission of Inquiry on Industrial Democracy, Chairman Lord Bullock; Cmnd. 6706, p. 13-15. This is why Trades Unions like nationalisation and dislike small business.

B

traditions—and will be locked in one overriding conflict with the older unions since they will not desire to assume the burden of providing open ended support for industries which, it will become ever clearer, are declining on a permanent basis.

Straddling the two groups will be the most immediately powerful group of all—workers in the essential nationalised industries. At one end, such as the power station operators, their instincts and culture are likely to be more in line with the new middle class unionism; at the other, railways and mines, they will continue to share the characteristics of industries in decline.

9. *Corporatism and its Effect*

The result will be that the movement to corporatism which has been quietly under way in Britain since the First World War—much advanced by the industrial direction necessary for the conduct of that war and its successor—will massively advance as other groups attempt to protect themselves against the power of the older manual workers' unions. In the process the homogeneous Trades Union movement is likely to disintegrate, since once nearly all workers are organised, the fiction that collective bargaining is anything other than a competition amongst and between workers will no longer be maintainable. In that sense, once everyone is unionised, the special significance of unions will disappear as conflicting organised interests cancel each out. The first loser in the process is likely to be those who cannot join or will not join an organisation; the second, the traditional Trades Union barons; and the third, representative democracy and the free media, which both rely for their power and independence on a theory of individual allegiance to a common good, not duty to a corporate representative. The Member of Parliament will be under pressure to convert himself from being the representative of all the interests of a territorial area to being the delegate of a sectional interest (and electoral reforms will be urged to make this easier); the editor will find himself under the same pressure to give up his commitment to objectivity in favour of a commitment to the representation of one interest or another.

All this will imply fundamental shifts in political allegiance and in the form of our government, to which we will return later.

10. *Centralisation and Technology.*

Other centripetal forces derive from technology. Just as more complex weaponry meant a standing army trained with artillery, and therefore an increase in the power of the state, so also system industry, winning huge advances in efficiency from large scale technology in electricity generation, telecommunications and other fields, leads naturally to centralised monopolistic corporations bureaucratically run. The power these system industries give not only to the state which normally owns or licenses them, but also to the few who run them, may have to be controlled as rigorously as ever were standing armies in successfully democratic countries. Otherwise, society may come to see the economic gains from the system as more than outweighed by the political costs of giving tyrannical power to electricity workers or miners. The choice will be: either, paramilitary discipline for such workers and managers; or, less dependence on the system, and more on private or community generators and other services. In the immediate future the latter is the more feasible course, and is one which governments should encourage.

11. *A Nuclear Economy?*

One technological advance in particular will interlink with politics. If Britain is not to dissipate its new found resource of off-shore oil up the chimneys of power stations in the next twenty years, we will need some increase in our civil nuclear capacity. This is inevitable even if we now turn serious resources on to the search for means of using other sources of energy which are available. Two such alternative sources—wind and tide—are, incidentally, exceptionally abundant around our North Atlantic islands. Nonetheless, even with oil, even with coal, even with some progress towards alternative sources, our existing substantial civil nuclear programme will be bound to increase by the end of the century, even if less dramatically than in, say, the USA or West Germany.

The spread of nuclear technology and materials has considerable political implications, of which we have been lucky to have careful early warning from Sir Brian Flowers in the Report of the Royal Commission on Environmental Pollution[9] and from Lord Rothschild.[10] These implications are threefold. In ascending order of importance they are, first, a further increase in the permanence of our dependence on a unified electricity system, since nuclear power stations are bound to be very large, their output manageable only by a huge distribution grid.

Second, all nuclear power stations, of whatever design, produce highly toxic radioactive waste products. Some of these, at least in the present state of technology, can only be disposed of by storing them in shielded vaults—sometimes in solid form, sometimes under water—and leaving them unattended for hundreds and, in some cases, thousands of years. This puts into the political system an unprecedented requirement for stability over time— and over time on an enormous scale in terms of the life of political institutions. Even for the wastes with relatively short half-lives, such as Strontium-90 and Caesium-137, it will be necessary to ensure their safekeeping for several centuries—say, for a period equivalent to that between the Battle of Bosworth Field and Queen Elizabeth II's Silver Jubilee. And those are the short-lived problems. Plutonium and Americium have isotopes with half-lives measured in thousands of years. To land this responsibility on succeeding generations is to make assumptions about future stability for which history offers no precedents.[11]

The storage of wastes, serious though it is, is not the most alarming problem. After all, there is a reasonable chance that the increasing problem of the storage of nuclear wastes will generate a technology for their safe disposal. The third, and the worst problem, as usual, is a human one—the problem of the misuse of materials and technology.

There are two stages in the nuclear fuel cycle when material may be extracted and used for weapons. At the stage where

[9] 'Nuclear Power and the Environment', Sixth Report of the Royal Commission on Environmental Pollution, London 1976.
[10] 'Nuclear Power for Good or Evil?' *The Times*, 27 September 1976, reprinted in *Meditations of a Broomstick* (Collins, 1977, p. 148-155).
[11] Flowers, op. cit., p. 80-81, 131-164. In the words of the Report, p. 80 'In considering arrangements for dealing safely with such wastes man is faced with time scales that transcend his experience.'

Uranium-238, a safe material, is 'enriched' by increasing above natural levels the proportion in it of Uranium-235, a fissile material, it would be possible to remove some of the slightly enriched mixture and further enrich it to the level needed for bomb manufacture. The technology of enrichment, once only possible in huge plants, is now becoming increasingly simple and feasible for groups with access only to laser technology and the sorts of sums of money which an Amin or a Gaddafi might make available.

Second, the waste products of nuclear reactors of normal thermal design include Uranium-235 itself, and Plutonium, an even more fissile (and toxic) substance. One reactor, indeed, the so-called Fast Breeder, has been designed to use this waste Plutonium as its basic fuel, and, if thought desirable, to produce more, requiring stockpiles of it and transportation. Because of the nature of the reactions in a nuclear pile, it is scientifically impossible exactly to predict the output of fissile materials to be expected; thus uncertainty is at once imported into any system of stock control.

The combination of the very much more widespread use, transportation and stocking of Plutonium and Uranium-235, with the difficulty of achieving a totally convincing audit, makes it a very real possibility that terrorist or criminal groups will at some time gain access to enough to build a bomb for purposes of nuclear blackmail.

Indeed, already in 1978, there is no way a government anywhere in the world, receiving such a threat, could be sure that it was not genuine. Nor could any nation, in dispute with any other, given the lead which the Indians have provided in turning civil nuclear capacity to the production of bombs, be sure that proliferation had not presented its opponent with a nuclear arsenal.

If anything ever forces on the human race effective international or non-national, policy, it will be experience of nuclear terrorism and proliferation. In the meantime, however, states will react by claiming that the only protection is vastly increased surveillance of possible terrorists, tougher measures for the internal defence of nuclear materials, and a limitation of the liberties of those who work in nuclear installations along military lines. These measures may or may not work. That they will be tried is certain, since they tend in the natural direction for a state bureaucracy—namely towards increase of its power.

Facing such developments, there is nothing sentimental about the Conservative's urgency in his demands for a lessening of the power of the nuclear lobby[12] in the British establishment and for serious research into alternative energy sources, using the revenues of North Sea oil. A tolerable political future requires both.[13]

[12] If you want really to terrify yourself about the prospects ahead of us, read some of the letters from the leaders of the British Atomic Energy Authority dismissing the dangers as trivial—*The Times* letter page, 1976 and 1977, passim.

[13] The energy debate has been greatly enlivened recently by the intervention of Britain's (and perhaps the world's) two most distinguished astronomers, Sir Fred Hoyle and Sir Martin Ryle. The former argues (*Energy or Extinction*, Heinemann, London 1977) in brilliant, even Swiftian style, that since the Russians appear to have most of the significant reserves of hydrocarbons, opposition in the West to nuclear energy (our only hope of independence) is in the interests of, if not inspired by, the Kremlin. The West, he points out, has a great deal of extractable Uranium, and there is Thorium everywhere. But there *are* genuine fears about the nuclear future, not inspired by the agents of Russia. $2 + 2$ might still $= 4$, even if it happened for some purpose to be in Mr. Breznev's interest that it was so. Professor Ryle, on the other hand, less conspiratorial but more quixotic, puts his faith in windmills.

CHAPTER FOUR

Countervailing Forces to the Growth of Government

1. Kicking the Bureaucracy.

The growth of the state will not go unchallenged. For just as the politician who claims to know how to produce long-term economic growth is misleading us, so is the politician who claims to know how to manage the state corporations and bureaucracies which constitute the expanding state. It is a most marked phenomenon of modern politics that the cry 'the government must act' is accompanied by a counterpoint of increasing hostility to those arms of government which attempt the requested action. The people may will the ends, but every opinion poll shows that they do not will the means as represented by the Inland Revenue, the nationalised industries, local and central government bureaucracies, and the leaders of Confederation of British Industry or Trades Union Congress whose final incorporation into the extended state is only delayed by the fact that the relevant leaders are loth to gain for themselves the general unpopularity of being government men.

Resistance—sometimes physical resistance[1]—already manifests itself in a thousand community and other groups up and down the land which are mostly dedicated to showing that it is only the incompetence of the bureaucracy which is responsible for the particular shambles under investigation—and that what is wanted is government action. It is very likely that such resistance will become rapidly more formidable, with more industrial strikes directly against government policy, tax avoidance increasing to the point where it will dignify itself as a tax strike, and

[1] Notable recent examples of physical resistance have been the battles on the proposed site of a new airport in Japan and a nuclear reactor site in France. More will follow.

other manifestations of 'respectable' opposition to government plans.

2. *The Failure of Bureaucratism.*

Why is this hostility to expanding government so marked? Why is the government bureaucrat the butt of every joke and the object of such widespread hostility? The answer lies in the fact that just as social democracy and its Conservative equivalent, based on the promise to deliver growth, were crushed by the fact that growth cannot be delivered to order, so statism in its various forms is crushed by the fact that no one has yet constructed a practical theory which says how government bureaucracy should work successfully. Thus, as such bureaucracies expand into increasingly important areas of the citizen's life, the fact that they often do not work well becomes apparent to millions of people who had not expected such failure. Often enough, they work so badly that disappointment soon becomes anger.

What are the criteria for the successful working of such bureaucracy—and why is it so difficult to invent a sensible theory of bureaucracy to ensure successful working? A summary list of necessary virtues might be that government organisations should serve their clients at a speed and with a courtesy comparable with private-enterprise organisations (by which the citizen's standards will be set); that, since the citizen has compulsorily to pay for them, the bureaucracies should have waste-controlling mechanisms which are effective and visible; that, since they are normally monopolies, pressures other than those of competition should be invented to maintain efficiency and to provide an equivalent of free enterprise's accountability to shareholders, workers and the market; and, perhaps above all, that enjoying as they do the support of a Leviathan state, they should have highly developed procedures for ensuring that they do not use this terrible power against the individual citizen in ways against which he cannot easily and effectively appeal if he thinks himself the victim of abuse of power.

In so far as we have a theory of bureaucracy in Britain, it rests on the now inadequate base of accountability to Parliament. The theory (long dead in reality) is that responsibility for the failure of some Gas Board official or junior clerk in Health and

Social Security will be accepted by an individual Minister, or by an individual Permanent Under-Secretary,[2] whose fear of such an event will force him to be so vigilant that an effective check against such failures is instituted. The theory is, of course, nonsense. Not since 1954 has a Minister resigned as a result of a mistake by one of his own immediate officials—and then most of his less squeamish colleagues thought him eccentric to go.[3] And when did a Permanent Under-Secretary *ever* go for like cause? No Minister with any brazenness about him need fear such an end to his career now if his civil servants make a mistake —let alone if some government agency for which he is formally accountable, like a nationalised industry, does so. As to the Boards of the latter, so lowly paid are they that it is now often a very difficult task to find anyone to do the job at all, which hardly encourages Ministers to sack the members they have : nor do the Boards themselves, as statutory monopolies for the most part, face competition, falling share prices, take-over, and the salutory arrival of Sir Arnold Weinstock.

To all intents and purposes, there is no accountability, and no theory of organisation. There is no military discipline—which would be one way to do it, and which, in softened and modified civil form, was the way in which the old, small Whitehall departments were run. The new bureaucracies are too big for that, and would not accept it. They cannot, with some exceptions to which we will return, be run by self-imposed disciplines as co-operatives—because they are monopolists and spenders of other people's money and have to be accountable for their use of both. They are without a theory of discipline, of accountability, or of organisation.

Even accounting for money is not enough. Accountability only for expenditure involves the judgement 'was this a reasonable amount to spend for such and such a degree of efficiency?'— better than nothing, and useful for avoiding corruption, but in-

[2] Permanent Under-Secretaries have their own separate accountability to Parliament for the expenditure of money, which can be a useful check for the Civil Service on a Minister casual with money. Sir Peter Carey played this card in 1975 in an attempt to limit Mr Wedgwood Benn's prodigality in disbursing money to co-operatives, which had at that time taken his fancy.

[3] Sir Thomas Dugdale, now Lord Crathorne, resigned in 1954 over the Crichel Down affair.

B*

108237

volving unproveable value judgements or dangerous comparisons
of like with unlike. How was the Department to know whether
money was being wasted on some aspect of Concorde's programme? Or how highly trained and paid primary school
teachers should be? Or how much planning there should be in
the hospital service? There is no clear answer; so all the objectives become merely parts of the bureacratic *status quo* to be
fought for by the bureaucrats who live off them and who will
gain by increase in their departments. What exists must get
bigger; there is no relevant cost-cutting ethos. Financial limits
merely contain an unaccountable and un-self-regulating organisation within bounds; they do not provide the motivation for
making the organisation meet the criteria for success we listed
above.

No one knows how to run bureaucracies. Bureaucracies are
increasing. No wonder the public thinks something is wrong.

3. *Britain and Europe*
We end this section where we began it—with the implications
for Britain of the foreign context. Dangers from the decaying
Russian Empire and increasing strains of readjustment between
the West and the populous nations are likely to inject a new
urgency into the movement towards regional groupings of the
older industrial countries. Under the shadow of Russia, political
weakness in one country will be of urgent importance to its
neighbours and allies. Increasingly, the short-term advantage
to be gained by one country, which may happen to be temporarily stronger, standing out from, say, co-ordinated European
policy on the decline of shipbuilding or car manufacture in
Europe will soon be seen to be far less than the danger to that
same country derived from corresponding collapse by whichever
partner happens to be weakest in that sector. What is more, the
maximisation of trade between the industrialised countries in
manufactured goods will postpone decline of those industries in
so far as a self-sufficient economic system, which could be
effectively protected by tariffs, could be approached. In so far as
this happens, the exclusion of cheap third-world goods will
prevent the populous nations earning anything with which to
pay for the West's food surplus, and international tension will

be heightened. This tension itself will add further impetus to the West's huddling together for defensive purposes and to the growth of a unified European foreign and defence policy. Taken together with the inevitable demand of an elected European Parliament that it should have something to do, and some power with which to do it, these positive, co-operative, and negative, defensive, forces are likely to lead to a new movement towards development of the European Community. The fact remains, however, that no new state or new centralised European authority will be able to challenge the power of national parliaments until it has its own capacity for enforcement; if it relies on national parliaments and national police for enforcement, it will remain secondary to the national unit in any conflict of interest between the two. Thus, in spite of far greater European co-ordination of industrial, political, military and trading policies, it is likely that in the year 2000 European policy will remain the sum of co-ordinated national policies. You cannot build adherence to a new state with a few years of somewhat uninspired propaganda; you cannot take away ultimate political power from a traditional holder of it unless, in the end, you are willing to outface whatever actual force is available to him. You *can* persuade people to co-operate to achieve common interests and to pool resources to do it; but that is a very different matter.

The greatest danger to the vision of effective European co-operation is the over-ambition of proponements of what amounts to a truly integrated European state. The disastrous doctrine that stealthy alignment of all sorts of regulations, major and minor, in the individual nations will somehow breed a common 'European consciousness'—seen as the epiphenomenon of standardised styles of administration—has already done enough to damage popular trust in the benevolence of the existing European Community and done much, by raising public hostility, to hinder co-operation on necessary areas such as defence.

Even worse—and potentially actually dangerous in terms of internal European conflict—would be an attempt to unite Europe by giving the European Parliament formal powers as if it was the Parliament of an already existing super-nation and hoping that trans-European national bonds would grow as a result. This danger is real, because the institutions of the EEC are much subject to Parkinson's Law. We will therefore see the *form* of European integration increasingly in dispute at the same time as the need for it is growing, and as the wrong route on which we are launched raises predictably strong hostility. The net result may be—and perhaps should be—a new start in Europe, a Second Foundation, from a different approach, and on a basis less like traditional state-building, than that embodied in the Treaty of Rome. Particularly if countries with highly fragile democratic traditions, such as Greece, Turkey and Spain, are to join the Community, the high ambitions, covert or overt, of the federalists must give way to an attempt to align what is alignable—namely defence and international trade policy, and some internal services. Allegiance to the old nations, may, in its own time decline, as we will argue further later; but the attempt to construct a new European nation from County Clare to Mount Ararat to take their place is a pipedream. A decentralised Empire—once; but to attempt to build a unitary nation out of such heterogeneous materials is to misunderstand what is meant by nationality.

4. *Political Demands: Summary*

So which, in the more conventional categories of electoral politics will be the issues of increasing importance in the next period—and which will be those whose importance declines?

In foreign affairs, the first problem will be of mounting tension in world trade, with battles over tariffs reflecting an attempt by the earlier industrial nations to hold manufacturing industries within their borders. International migration will be feared by the food producers and only half-heartedly opposed by the over-populated. The West will have to decide its attitude to Russian satellites seeking independence—how near to go to helping them without endangering world peace. In Europe, the argument will rage between amalgamators, who will seek to build a unitary state on the basis of institutions, and co-ordinators, who will demand new institutions more effectively capable of aligning sovereign national policies. There will be plenty of danger of major war—particularly in the Far East between Russia and China—and certainty of lesser regional wars.

At home, the struggles of declining industries to maintain employment by tariffs and by direct subsidy, will make issues of creating jobs paramount and will continue to raise problems between regions of the country affected very differently; agriculture, science and high technology, already concentrated most successfully in the southern half of England, will protect the prosperity of that part of the kingdom. In the declining cities unemployment will tend to rise, and with it housing will deteriorate and crime increase. Urban stress is likely in many places to have a racial flavour. At the same time, restrictions on land use outside cities should become tougher, forcing a reversal, in the end, of migration from cities; the disastrous state of the poorer parts of big towns is likely to encourage the returning middle class to concentrate itself in clearly defined areas, producing marked divisions between rich and poor districts.

In terms of political organisation, since no one can think of a way of breaking the power of traditional manual workers' unions over other workers, the other workers will organise and thus create countervailing powers; Parliament as at present constituted will be in danger of eclipse as a focus for national discussion and the resolution of conflict in an increasingly corporate state. Government will continue to grow—and continue to become more unpopular. The freedom of the media will be under more and more pressure. Underlying everything, food prices and prices of other scarce goods demand for which will be subject to the relentless increase in world population, will continue to rise; growth of real living standards will be problematic, and those who promise it discredited; and the national mood, in the face of a world not changing our way, grim and perhaps politically dangerous.

PART II

Political Possibilities

CHAPTER ONE

The Political Response

What are likely to be the main political responses offered to the electorate in reaction to a world changing in the way we have described? And which of them offers the best chance of mitigating or curing the unpleasant problems which, on our present course, we seem likely to encounter?

1. The Decline of Social Democracy and the Rise of Communism

First, of course, we may expect to see the representatives of those whose jobs in traditional industries become less and less secure claim that this is because of a failure of free enterprise and that it could be avoided by State ownership. Already shipbuilding, mining, a good section of motor car, aircraft and aircraft engine industries have got into this position: no doubt there will be demands that large sections of, for example, the remaining engineering, textiles, electrical, chemical and printing industries follow, probably together with financial institutions blamed for the failure of free enterprise to revivify these dinosaurs. However, since the problem will be nothing to do with the failure of one method of financing investment or another, and much to do with the irresistible rise of cheaper manufacturing elsewhere in the world, this will have little effect on anything except to transfer the blame for unemployment and collapse from foreigners (where in a sense it belongs) to the home government who will be the new owners. Since these older manufacturing areas, and their associated Trades Unions, form the backbone of the Labour Party—which is historically the same age as they are, is their creation, and is largely controlled by them—the Labour Party is likely to become the minority party representing those declining interests: the party of the unemployed in Scotland, the north-east, Lancashire, and parts of the Midlands. It will have as its objectives the erection of tariffs to protect its constituents; and the siphoning of subsidies from the rest of the economy to support them. However, as governments, even those controlled by the Labour Party, show no greater ability than anyone else to reverse the trend of history in favour of these industries and their workers, the activists of that party (drawn from the declining industrial sector and the decaying city centres) are likely to come more and more into conflict with their national Parliamentary leaders who, presumably, will remain committed to trying to attract the wider support needed to win elections.

Thus the underlying trend of the Labour movement will be further and further to the kind of socialism represented by workers' control in opposition to 'State capitalism'—since State capitalism will be blamed for its inability to combat industrial decline, and workers' control represents the only alternative remaining.

In the cities, similar extreme socialism will provide a theoretical justification for direct action of various sorts—such as ghetto rent strikes, police no-go areas, and abandonment of the state education system in favour of 'community controlled' schools.

The Labour Party of government has been based on a commitment to state-guaranteed employment, an approach to the equalisation of possessions, government spending, and the abolition of poverty. It will be seen to have failed to achieve the first or the last, and will find the new unionism of those groups formed to prevent the erosion of differentials preventing it from doing the second, and public hostility rising against the bureaucracy spawned by the third. It is likely, therefore, to go into rapid decline from which the allegiance of the remaining social democrats to 'moderation' (that is, warfare against the activists) and growth (impossible to deliver) will not rescue it.

Only Marxist-Leninist Communism—at war both with 'Trotskyite' and syndicalist extreme groups, and with the remaining social democrats—will promote on the left a philosophy with the confidence to govern and a strategy for the attainment of power. To the fallacies of this philosophy and the dangers it regularly brings of the misuse of power, we will return: we have already mentioned the difficulties it is likely to face in its Russian Empire, the decline of which should affect its world-wide prestige. But in the medium-term future, in Britain as in Europe, the left with the confidence to go for government is increasingly likely to be the Communist left in its traditional form.

2. *Neo-Liberalism.*

A second line, offered by some people within the Conservative Party, and, most likely, by new small parties based on newly-collectivised middle class interests (if changes in the electoral system facilitate their emergence) will be to offer a return to the most recent plausible golden age. The golden age will be that of nineteenth-century political and industrial free trade, the heyday of the joint stock company identified, somewhat oddly, with the economics of Adam Smith (who believed in fact that the joint stock company was unlikely to be compatible with his eighteenth century model of a self-rectifying economy).[1] In a later chapter, we will discuss the merits and demerits of this approach as a political cry for Conservatives. Here, we need to attempt an assessment of its likely political relevance.

First, in its analysis of what will be happening in the world, the revitalised Liberalism will have a great deal more to offer than disintegrating socialism. The Cobdens of the future will correctly observe that it is not because of the wickedness of capitalists or the treason of Social Democrats that motor cars, ships and electrical consumer goods will be more cheaply produced in Indonesia, India, Brazil, China, and Nigeria, but because workers there, willingly or under compulsion, will be working for something much more consonant with Ricardo's iron law of wages (namely, that the 'natural price' of labour is the cost of labourers' subsistence)[2] than the inhabitants of Glas-

---

[1] 'Negligence and profusion, therefore must always prevail, more or less, in the management of the affairs of such a Company.' Adam Smith, *An Enquiry into the Nature and Causes of the Wealth of Nations*, ed. Campbell, Skinner and Wood, 2 vols., (Clarendon Press, Oxford, 1976) p. 741. See also p. 756.

[2] 'The natural price of Labour is that price which is necessary to enable the labourers, one with another, to subsist and to perpetuate their race, without either increase or diminution.'; David Ricardo, *Works and Correspondence*, Vol. 1, ed. P. Sraffa and M. H. Dobb, Chapter 5, p. 93.

gow or Liverpool. The latter, it will be rightly pointed out, are
seeking merely to transfer wealth created by others in Britain
and Europe to themselves by political force via pressures exercised on governments. Less convincingly, it will be argued that
if only they would allow their real wages to fall back, they would
become competitive again and capital would naturally flow to
them and all—after, doubtless, a difficult time not unrelated,
in the view of some of these Liberals, to a deserved period of
punishment—would be well. On the issue of the city centres
some (but very few) of this school will have the courage to follow
through the implications of their economic beliefs to the necessary
conclusions that the free movement of capital must be matched
by the free movement of immigrant labour; others, like Enoch
Powell in the past, will look to their electoral base and find
sophistries to allow blame for the collapse of many urban economies to fall on the very arrival the cheap labour which they
ought to welcome, that arrival being, of course, part of the
evidence of collapse, and not a cause of it.

   In government, this Liberalism will work as a frustration-
machine rather in the same way as will the failed State-socialism
of the Labour Party and the millenarianism of its attendant
leftist sects. Equally, its failure will breed conspiracy theory (in
this demonology, wicked Communists and the treason of Conservatives replace the capitalists and Social Democrats of the
left's nightmares). Its failure will derive from the fact that in a
world where there is likely to be a surplus of manufactured goods,
there will be no reason at all for new capital to seek out the
decayed industrial archaeology of Merseyside or Clydeside, with
its politics of workers control, its race problems, and its attachment to the past, for new plants; and even if it did, it is a betting
certainty that the new factories of the future will not take up
more than a fraction of the labour employed in the old industries
unless the workers are willing to surrender themselves to the
subsistence levels of their new rivals abroad which, faced with
the continuing prosperity of much of the country, and urged
on by their political representatives, they will be most unlikely
to do. So it will either be large numbers of cheap jobs—which
will not be accepted—or a few highly paid jobs—which will only
marginally affect the situation.

   The truth of the matter is, that the Liberal nineteenth-century golden age is a chimaera : its free trade rested on the ability of British military and political power to sell mass-produced goods in markets from which competitors were excluded, and in many of which there would have been only minimal competition anyway; to balance the even then existing trade deficit with the power given us by a tremendous advantage of naval strength and merchant-marine capacity to conduct world trade in British ships, shipped and insured by British service industries; and to provide for ourselves privileged access, at privileged prices, to many essential raw materials. Our population expanded in response to the wealth which our politicians and our military force had brought us; now, we face the consequences : an island populated to levels only supportable in full industrial employment as part of the global political system which stimulated the growth of that population. If we are to have Cobden and Bright back, we must have Palmerston and India too.

Sadly, our new liberals will not have much to say to protectionist Trades Unions, poujadist small business, shippers and persecutors of illegal immigrants, Minister in charge of nationalised industries, unemployed Merseysiders, or the millions employed by expanding government—except to tell them that, if only all of them did not exist, the world would be a better place. The description of how most people behave in the market-place which Liberal economics offers is right and useful, in so far as it is based on sensible observation of what people prefer; it is certainly much more practical than anything produced by the Marxists, whose economic generalisations are based on what people ought to prefer. It enables us to predict some of the future areas of tension and trouble. But the market-place is not where most people live, most of their lives, and it is not where the most important events in life take place. The political advice, derived from Liberal economic theory, to those seeking in all manner of ways outside the market to obtain goods, or prevent others having goods, which are not always saleable, or to those charged with governing nations of such people, leaves governors naked and its own adherents always frustrated at the distance between their model of the world and reality. A political philosophy, to be of use, must offer explicitly the theory of government, consent, and community that the eighteenth and nineteenth century Liberals were able to assume since they inherited, and relied on, the continuance from the past of a substructure older than and independent of their theory. As Fred Hirsch says:

> First, full participation in nineteenth century liberal capitalism was confined to a minority—the minority that had reached material affluence before liberal capitalism had set the masses on the path of material growth. Second, the system operated on social foundations laid under a different order of society.[3]

We, however, must seek a philosophy which will allow us to provide fuller participation with social foundations too—and to do it, we will argue after, we will need more than the Liberal philosophy can give us.

3.   *Conservatism*

Increasing government, forever spreading increasing hostility towards itself; the final death of the political consensus which tried to avoid questions of redistribution—and hence a new/old friction between class; an external world which will increase our industrial difficulties at home and involve us in tremendous global conflicts of interest. We are heading into a very dangerous period. The rival philosophies of civilised Conservatism, inspired by Burke, and morally-based reform represented by Grey, just steered us through an equally dangerous period after the Napoleonic wars, without the collapse into tyranny or anarchy which might have been feared as well then as now. Do we have political philosophies which will help us to safety again?

The answer is 'yes'. There is a Conservative tradition relevant to the next twenty-five years. The Conservative Party needs to disentangle the various threads of its inheritance to find those which are useful, and then embody that tradition in policies which will together offer a strategy. Let us now turn to an examination of that Conservative tradition.

---

[3] Fred Hirsch: Op. Cit., p. 11.

CHAPTER TWO

The Conservative Tradition

For three hundred years, a continuous tradition has existed of an approach to politics which urges the maintenance of old institutions as the repositories of distilled tradition; the conduct of private and public life according to moral rules, usually religiously based; the preservation of an unchallengeable state power, to be the sole legitimate user of force within the nation and to be the shield of the weak and the avenger of injustice; and which, of two great evils, fears anarchy more than tyranny.

This tradition very often finds its most eloquent expressions in the approval of social stability and order implicit in the work of a novelist like Jane Austen; in poetry which relies for its effect on the complex echoes which words can evoke in a society where cultural continuity still has power, as perhaps does that of Coleridge or Eliot; or in the thought of a philosopher and critic like Trilling who suggests that without an underlying cultural unity the possibility of writing a novel which is anything other than a private psychological exercise may be lost.

Inherent in it, sometimes as religious faith, sometimes as empirical assumption, is a belief in original sin, if you like, or the imperfectability on earth of man. The tradition believes, with Hobbes, that there is nothing inherently noble about the savage, nor desirable about the state of nature. The parable of William Golding's *Lord of the Flies* is of this tradition; or, again, that of Orwell's *Animal Farm*: neither without the restraints of civil society is man to be trusted—nor is any such society, however organised, capable of changing man's nature. It approves Marx's relativism when he argues that cultural values will shift with different kinds of society (though thinks him naive to imagine that only the economic organisation of society is relevant and silly to exclude his own views from the theory) and takes the far more thoroughgoing relativism of Xenophanes[1] two and a half millenia earlier to be more intellectually respectable.

Nothing imagined as proven by man can be taken as fixed for ever, however useful for the time being; nothing claimed for any theory should be treated with other than scepticism. Hume is of the tradition when he shows that no proof about what does or does not exist has certainty in the sense that a deduction about logical abstractions may have one answer which is certainly true.[2] Johnson is of the tradition when he refutes Berkeley's proof that what we directly perceive is mental, and therefore has no reality in the external world, by kicking a stone: no logical disproof, but a warning that Berkeley's conclusion changes nothing in the way we must live.[3]

Scepticism, fear of anarchy, and recognition that the imperfections of man stem from his nature, lead to caution about social change and a belief that society is to be compared to an organism, (as Burke tends to do),[4] which is merely a picturesque way of saying that society is best thought of as something infinitely complex whose interrelations we do not understand, and which we can kill more easily than we can create. They lead to a fear of change based on current theory because current theory is certain to be imperfect and the imperfection may be a critical one. They lead to a trust in well tried rules of thumb; people of this turn of mind note how similar the basic few moral rules of all societies are to one another, and take them either as hints

[1] 'But if cattle and horses or lions had had hands, or were able to draw with their hands and do the works that men can do, horses would draw the forms of the gods like horses, and cattle like cattle, and they would make their bodies such as they each had themselves.' Xenophanes, Fragment 15, Diels-Kranz Fragmente der Vorsokratische (Berlin, 1922), translated by G. Kirk and J. E. Raven in *The Presocratic Philosophers* (Cambridge, 1962), p. 169. It did not seem to occur to Marx that dissatisfied German-Jewish Hegelian philosophers, given hands with which to write, made up a Communist theory very much in their own image.

[2] 'Nothing is demonstrable unless the contrary implies a contradiction. Nothing that is distinctly conceivable implies a contradiction. Whatever we conceive as existent, we can also conceive as non-existent. There is no being, therefore, whose non-existence implies a contradiction. Consequently there is no being whose existence is demonstrable. I propose this argument as entirely decisive . . .' David Hume, *Dialogues Concerning Natural Religion* (Hafner, New York, 1966), p. 58.

[3] Boswell, *Life of Dr Johnson* (J. M. Dent, London 1958), Vol. 2, p. 292.

[4] See, for example, the quotation on page 62, below.

revealed by God of the way to salvation, or distillations of immense experience of an underlying human nature through time and across space, and of the most sensible way of ordering human relations. In either case they see these rules—whether dignified as God's law, or regarded as the grandest of all rules of thumb—as far as more worthy of unquestioning support than any ephemeral attacks on them. Nor do they worry that there will always be argument about the exact list of virtues to be advanced by such rules, since they find a comparison of Aristotle, Christ, Buddha, Marcus Aurelius, Mahomet, Aquinas, Luther, and Marx provides a perfectly workable list of general virtues: courage, honesty, fairness, kindness, loyalty, humour and humility—which is anyway known perfectly well to any normal person who has never bothered considering the subject, just as it was to his equivalent in Aristotle's day who never got around to reading the Nichomachean Ethics.

Finally, just as language and morality themselves inhere in groups, and are impossible to the isolated individual, so does all man's hope of self-fulfilment depend on his membership of society so organised, and on such a scale, that his need for his fellows is balanced by his need for solitude. Neither group nor individual can sensibly be treated as primary; man alone—except in so far as he retains traces of a group—is nothing: the group as an abstract concept apart from its members is only a diagram. The Conservative tradition rightly balances the two and sees a sound nation as one where independent communities flourish under the protective and judicial eye of a supreme State not owned by any one interest, and not afraid when necessary to use its power. This concept of community we will explore further in a later chapter: along with scepticism about the ability of man to embody final truth in compulsory social organisations, it is essential to the Conservative tradition.

This is the tradition which, in politics, is the Tory or the Conservative tradition. Since its strength lies not in a descent from explicit political theory, but in an attitude towards the nature of man and of society, it tends not to be a tradition based on the works of great political philosophers—there could never be a Conservative bibliography as there could be a Marxist (which is why Marxism is easier to teach in schools). But the Conservative tradition has its respectable wordsmiths.

The words may be Bolingbroke's in 1747 :
'Instead of abetting the divisions of his people, the Patriot King will endeavour to unite them, and to be himself the centre of their union : instead of putting himself at the head of one party in order to govern his people, he will put himself at the head of his people in order to govern, more properly to subdue, all parties.'[5]

They may be Burke's in 1790 :
'Our political system is placed in a just correspondence and symmetry with the order of the world, and with the mode of existence decreed to a permanent body composed of transitory parts—wherein, by the disposition of a stupendous wisdom, moulding together the great mysterious incorporation of the human race, the whole, at one time, is never old, or middle-aged, or young, but, in a condition of unchangeable constancy, moves on through the varied tenor or perpetual decay, fall, renovation and progression. Thus, by preserving the method of Nature in the conduct of the State, in what we improve we are never wholly new, in what we retain we are never wholly obsolete . . .'[6]

They may be Disraeli's in 1872 :
'Gentlemen, another great object of the Tory party, and one not inferior to the maintenance of the Empire, or the upholding of our institutions, is the elevation of the condition of the people . . .'[7]

They may be Lord Hugh Cecil's in 1912 :
'Conservatives defend the constitution, property and the existing social order, partly from the natural conservative love of what exists, partly from a dread of injustice threatened to individuals by advocates of revolutionary change. This resistance to injustice finds a moral basis in the religious principles inherited from the Tory adhesion to the Church . . .'[8]

They may be Oakeshott's in 1947 :
'The politician exists . . . first . . . to prevent concentrations of power which have the appearance of becoming dangerous . . . The second function is to take the initiative in seeking out the

[5] Bolingbroke, *The Idea of a Patriot King* (London 1775), p. 142.
[6] Edmund Burke, *Reflections on the Revolution in France* (Dent, London 1960), p. 31-2.
[7] Speech to the National Union of Conservative and Constitutional Associations, 24 June, 1872.
[8] Lord Hugh Cecil, *Conservatism* (London 1912), p. 245.

current mischiefs and maladjustments in a society and to set them right'.[9]

They may be Hailsham's in 1959:

'The Conservative intends that the most a politician can do is to ensure that some, and these by no means the most important, conditions in which the good life can exist are present, and more important still, to prevent fools from setting up conditions which make any approach to the good life impossible except for solitaries or anchorites'.[10]

Conservative policies vary over the years to meet varying challenges to the state's monopoly of legal force; to the state's right to see that the condition of its people is not sacrificed to political exploitation or to economic fashion; to the state's ability to defend itself from the encroachment of over-mighty subjects; or to meet new tests for the legitimising of its own authority. But the Conservative turn of mind has been easily recognisable behind the necessary shifts in policy: never afraid of swift state action to relieve injustice or defend the weak; always afraid of fashionable theory and of exclusive claims to the truth; always aware of the reality of irrationality and original sin; always frightened of the dark side of the human psyche dressed up in political clothes as Jacobinism, Bolshevism, Stalinism, Fascism or racism.

Taking part in a political process in order to keep its version of truth alive, it has always recognised the danger of faction within the nation, and aims to maintain a common national tradition within which faction can be contained; lacking trust in any man's ability to devise one final way to social settlement, it has not feared to borrow bits and pieces of political machinery from any available ideological factories, agreeing with Robert Nozick that 'it is helpful to imagine cavemen sitting together to think up what, for all time, will be the best possible society and then setting out to institute it', and with the import of his next rhetorical question 'Do none of the reasons that make you smile at this apply to us?'[11]

In short, there has always been in England a sceptical, careful, moral tradition in politics which has known an evil when it has

[9] Michael Oakeshott, *Contemporary British Politics* (*Cambridge Journal* 1947/48), p. 487.
[10] Quintin Hogg, *The Conservative Case* (Penguin 1959), p. 14.
[11] Robert Nozick, *Anarchy, State and Utopia* (Oxford 1974), p. 313-14.

seen one, and thought it a public duty to use state power where possible to eliminate such evil, as it would have thought it a private duty to use private resources to the same end, and which has stood out at various times against the pocketing of power by the Whig political mafia, against the abdication of its duty by the state under the influence of liberal economic theory, and against the attempt to turn one section of the people against the rest, and against the state, by Marxian socialism.

Where is that tradition now? One purpose of this book is to remind the Conservatives that by discovering the Liberal classics in their new and vigorous guise, in the writings of Professors Von Hayek, Friedman, and Nozick,[12] they have not discovered true Conservatism but true Liberalism; to maintain that the Conservative tradition (though it may cheerfully make use of these sages—and indeed of passages in Marx and Mao Tse-Tung) is nothing without a belief in a primary role for the community and a decisive role for the state, since direct action by modern successors to the Patriot King will be necessary to protect tolerable life whatever spontaneous order flowers from the soil of Viennese economics; and, above all, to remind Conservatives that no single intellectual system, learned from books, can match the subtlety of a society made up of the relationships of millions of people grouped in myriads of communities; and that it is the whole corpus of accumulated wisdom embodied in traditional patterns of life and, often, made manifest in the bricks and mortar of our old institutions—from scientific societies to country villages—to which we must look.

[12] See Bibliography for details of some of the politically influential books by these three.

CHAPTER THREE

Manipulating the Sovereign State

It would be absurd to argue that there is a continuous tradition within the Conservative Party of belief in the active exercise of State power on the basis alone of quotations from writers whom Conservatives revere. Their witness is important, since Conservatives, asked to identify their beliefs, very often define themselves in terms of allegiances to past heroes—or in terms of opposition to past villains. A Conservative may well say, when pressed to define his philosophy, that he is the sort of man who would have opposed Charles Fox or Gladstone or Aneurin Bevan and the sort of man who would have followed Pitt or Disraeli or the later Churchill. But a far more important witness is the reality of Conservative action over the centuries.

Again and again, Conservatives or Tories have, in power, grasped the levers of State power and set the machinery into effective action. When Whig corruption had become Whig torpor, it was Chatham and Pitt by decisive use of authority who mobilised the nation for war. Indeed, it is a recurrent feature of the history the Tory party that the nation understands that, in wartime, government needs to be in the hands of those who believe in the exercise of the State's authority and has often in such situations turned to the more decisive members of the Tory tradition.

Above all, consistently, throughout the nineteenth century, the Conservatives stood opposed to the abdication of power urged by those who found seductive the model, invented by the French physiocrats and perfected by Smith, James Mill, and Ricardo, of society as a self-rectifying economic machine. Tories would regard with horror the advice given to the future King Louis XVI by Quesnay. Asked by the Dauphin what he would do if he were king, the author of the Tableau Economique

answered, 'Nothing'—and became a hero of the Liberal tradition for ever.[1] Rather would Tories go along with de Jouvenel
in putting the blame for the subsequent slaughter in France and
chaos in Europe on the shoulders of those who took such slogans
to heart :

> 'The fall of the French monarchy at the end of the eighteenth
> century was certainly not caused by despotism on its part. A
> weaker government has rarely been seen and its financial
> difficulties were the sign of its weakness. The king did not
> feel himself strong enough either to raise enough money in
> new taxation or to cut down the scale of his liberalities by a
> like amount'.[2]

The same might go for the Roman Empire after Caracalla;
the Russian Empire before the First World War; or the Manchu
Empire under the Empress Dowager. And does this not strike
a chord in Britain since the Second World War?

Through the nineteenth century, then, Conservatives retained
the knowledge that the State had a right and a duty to preserve
its power in the face of the claims of allegedly inexorable economic laws. This is not to say that they were not sometimes on
the side of the capitalists against traditional powers in the land;
though his action may not be quite as obviously heroic as every
Liberal school book tells us, there was nothing un-Tory in Peel's
using the forces of free trade to lessen the power of the landed
interest when he repealed the Corn Laws in 1840. The doubt
remains, however, whether by depressing the income of that
majority of the population (perhaps 60% in 1840) who lived
directly or indirectly from the land, in order to cut the cost of
employing workers in the new cities, he did not merely cause his
opponent—the huge landowner—to change the shape of his
spots, into those of the industrial capitalist, while certainly
damaging in the long term good friends of the Tory nation, the
yeoman farmer and the small country gentleman, and with them,
thousands of rural communities in which the majority of the
population still, then, lived.

Disraeli's government followed a more subtle line—welcoming

---

[1] Eduard Heimann, *History of Economic Doctrines* (Oxford 1972), p. 52.
[2] B. de Jouvenel, Sovereignty : *An Enquiry into the Political Good* (London
1957), p. 80.

the rise of articulate organised labour to set against the power of the capitalist; understanding the inherent contradiction and hypocrisy of Liberal imperialism which, in order to reconcile the irreconcilables of self-determination and imperial domination, had to seek out ways of defining the subject peoples as deserving less than full human rights in order to avoid giving them those rights, and thereby laid the foundation for systematic racism. At least Conservatives, accepting that there could be a theory of benevolent authority not based on such sophistry, did not have to follow them down that path. Acts of Parliament of Disraeli's Government embodied the Tory's moral revulsion against some of the unacceptable faces of the capitalism of the day; Salisbury and Balfour did not hesitate to put the State's power into the scales on the side of better organisation of education and defence.

This is not to say that Conservatives were opposed to capitalism though they often distrusted it.[3] Believing in the widespread dissemination of property rights as an effective way of obtaining commitment by the individual to his community, and tenacity by the individual of his own rights against the misuse of power by over-mighty subjects or corrupt officials of the State, Conservatives have always believed that stable rules governing the free transfer of property should seldom be interfered with by Government. This is not because of any inescapable logical connection between property and a decent society : certainly there could be a society, protecting individuals and communities by other traditions, without private property;[4] it is because on the whole Conservatives accept the empirical argument of Aristotle that a property owning 'middle' in society is a powerful support for necessary continuity and a strong base for resistance to populist or authoritarian tyranny :

'The best form of political society is one where power is vested in the middle class, and, second . . . good government is attain-

[3] For example, Lord Henry Bentinck wrote a splendid slashing attack on the social divisiveness of Liberal economics in his *Tory Democracy* of 1918. I am grateful to J. H. Phipps for telling me about this book.
[4] It is, however, quite difficult to imagine one. Locke, in his Second Treatise of Government, Chapter 5, tries to persuade us that it is virtually impossible; he is nearly successful. Hegel, in his more opaque language, makes a case for the necessity of property to individual identity (Hegel, *Philosophy of Right*, trans. T. M. Knox, Oxford, 1967 p. 40 ff. See also *Phenomenology of Spirit*, trans. A. V. Miller, Oxford, 1977, p. 257 ff.

able in those states where there is a large middle class—large
enough, if possible, to be stronger than both of the other classes,
but at any rate large enough to be stronger than either of them
singly . . . It is therefore the greatest of blessings for a state
that its members should possess a moderate and adequate
property'.[5]

This is an argument Conservatives accept because it seems to
accord with what we observe of how people behave in societies
we know and have to deal with. It is an empirical judgement,
and a far cry from the fanaticism of those who claim to believe,
like Robert Nozick,[6] that so long as just rules of property transfer
are observed, whatever society ensues is to be accepted. No rules,
to start with, can be devised which will be universally accepted
as just (if you doubt it, read Nozick's brilliant attempt to devise
a set) and even if they could, no Tory is going to surrender his
right to correct an evil where he sees one because of an argument
that the evil he sees is an inevitable outcome of just rules : no
human action can be certainly predicted if we believe in free
will; and no system of rules will cover every situation. Newtonian
mechanics is a pretty model, but . . . light bends and $E=MC^2$
(until we find a better formula); Russelian logic and mathematics
seemed a complete system, but . . . Gödel showed that we can
never prove that a logical system is complete and self-consistent.
There will never be such a thing as a final explanation or a final
scientific model—those who seek one delude themselves like the
astrologers of the middle ages. No man's political or moral theory
can prevent us saying : I see something evil, and if I can I will
stop it, any more than a scientist's hypothesis can prevent other
scientists pursuing recalcitrant facts which cannot be explained
by it.

So the Conservative's attachment to property is empirical,
conditional, possible of dissolution. But it is strong enough to
withstand the contrary fallacy, Marxism : a theory combining
in a disastrous alliance the absurdities of historicist philosophy
with the categories of Liberal economics. The next chapter must
glance at the shift of balance which Marxism called forth in the
Tory tradition.

[5] Aristotle, *Politics*, 1295b-1296a, Trans. Sir Ernest Barker (Oxford 1962).
[6] *Anarchy, State and Utopia* (Blackwell, 1974), p. 150 ff.

CHAPTER FOUR

The Marxist Second Front

This essay does not attempt a history of the Conservative Party. My purpose is to attempt to show why the main elements of current Conservative philosophy came to be what they are, and to attempt to show that one, perhaps an element currently in danger of eclipse, is highly relevant to the problems we are likely to face next.

In historical terms, it would be quite wrong to give the impression that the main areas of nineteenth-century political dispute were economic or industrial—between Ricardian or Smithian economists on the one hand, and Tory or Socialist interventionists on the other. In fact, of course, religious issues, Ireland (often a special case of religious dispute), the franchise, and issues of war and peace abroad engaged the attention of the nineteenth century Houses of Parliament more deeply than economic affairs. Only with the Repeal of the Corn Laws at the beginning of Victoria's reign, and the controversies about tariff reform and Trades Unions at its end, does politics take a familiar modern form. As Lord Blake reminds us, the fact is easily forgotten today:

> ... when Ireland and religion no longer dominate the legislature, viz. the immense amount of political time which both subjects occupied throughout the nineteenth century. In modern times the great issues have been economic and social.[1] In those days they were religious and constitutional. The first parliament in which economic issues were dominant was that of 1900, thanks to Joseph Chamberlain's crusade for tariff reform.[2]

Thus I am well aware that to say that the Conservative Party

---

[1] Recently, of course, the Irish Question has returned in all its old bitterness.
[2] Blake, op. cit. p. 34.

C

began to face a new challenge from the 1870s onwards—a challenge from socialism revitalised by Marx—is not to describe the party politics of the day. The Conservative domination of the last decades of the century derived from Disraeli's achievement in making the party appear the natural protector of the middle-class property owner, Salisbury's effective organisation of this 'Villa Toryism', Liberal suicide over Ireland and, above all, Disraeli's establishment of the Conservatives as the national or patriotic party in an era of imperial pride and imperial nerves about rival empires. Nevertheless, thoughtful Conservatives knew that it was the socialist tide which represented the future, and reacted accordingly.

Balfour knew that the real portent of 1906 was not the Liberal working majority of nearly three hundred and fifty, but the fact that after the election there were fifty-two Labour members; Lord Hugh Cecil explored in 1912 the areas of philosophical coincidence between Conservative and Socialist, while Lord Henry Bentinck warned of the dire consequences for the Conservatives if their Party should become simply the party of the capitalists; and Baldwin spent his first quiet years in the House of Commons developing the language of class-reconciliation and talking to the Trades Union members of the Labour Party in the smoking-room.

More fundamentally, however, attention was bound to shift from the weaknesses of free-traders who believed in the minimum of Government to the dangers of socialists who believed that nothing was beyond the legitimate concern of governments. But it is important to see what is objectionable to the Conservative in socialism, and why.

First of all, there is nothing inherently absurd to many Conservatives (though fewer now) in the Hegelian framework of historical inevitability and historical cycles which Marx absorbed from his cultural background and with which his economic and political thinking is decorated. After all, Carlyle may have pleased Marx, but he also influenced many Conservatives; and even some whose primary commitment is to economic Liberalism: Enoch Powell described on BBC radio in 1970 the importance of Carlyle in his intellectual development:

'So there had been someone else who thrilled to German as I

did and could express in English—and in what English—all
that I felt about my new-found spiritual home'.[3]

Ricardo tended in some moods to believe that capitalism faced
a cycle ending in inevitable extinction—but is still thought of
as perhaps the most influential of Liberal economists; and certain
types of Christian (Teilhard de Chardin would be a modern
example) put forward theories of the development of God's will
towards man which are every bit as historicist as Marx. Intellectually disreputable as the concept of historical inevitability
may seem to many—and morally and governmentally quite use-
less as it certainly is—believers are not confined to Marxists or
to the left.

Thus it is not the concept of historical inevitability as such
which puts Marxist socialism into conflict with Conservative
thinking, since it is possible for many such theorists to leave a
place for the individual's apparent consciousness of free
will which, while meaning that the theory gives him little or
no help in day-to-day life, leaves open to argument all the old
questions of morality and personal action.

What was, and is, objectionable to Conservatives is the use
of the concept of historical inevitability to give believers greater
rights over their fellow men than non-believers. Like some austere
Calvinists or inquisitorial Catholics, those who understand the
direction of the cycle have a duty further to advance it; what
they do to non-believers, or to each other, in the process is of
no real significance. Thus by one jump—the identical jump
made by Hegel's Fascist descendants—the believers find themselves equipped with a philosophy which entitles them to make
no distinction between those who disagree with them and those
who are delaying the progress of all mankind towards the
promised land. Materialism prevents them from saying, like
some Christians in the past, that the soul of the tortured individual is actually benefited in another world; but the cry that
millions unborn will benefit from the present slaughter of
dissenters opens the gates to the torture chamber just as effectively.

[3] Quoted by Mark Bonham Carter in a review in *The Times* Literary
Supplement, 15.7.77.

So the Tory, sceptical of theory, firm in his understanding that he knows evil when he sees it, is back in the mood he was in when he found those who were sending six-year-olds to their deaths in the lead chimneys of Somerset defending themselves with the arguments of free trade.[4] If your theory pretends that it is inevitable that such children will go to their deaths—or the kulacs to theirs—or Solzhenitsyn to the Gulag Archipelago—too bad for your theory, Liberal or socialist. What is more, any decent theory of government will have to provide us with the rationale for stopping you, and the power to do it.

Thus historical inevitability, as used by Marxists in power, offends the first and most important instinct of the Tory: the belief that man is not God; that no social theory is more than a collection of interesting remarks which may sometimes be helpful, but must always be discarded in the face of obstinate fact. What is more, so convenient and so terrible is the weapon it provides to Marxist regimes, or to Marxists who seek power, that it is impossible not to see the theory as just a modern flowering of that dangerous old sophistry whose first appearance is in the mouth of Thrasymachus in Plato's *Republic*—namely the argument that 'might is right', that what governments can get away with, governments have a right to do.[5] This argument, destroyed by Plato two thousand three hundred years ago, reappearing with unpleasant regularity whenever a dictatorship arises which understands the value of intellectual window-dressing in maintaining itself, will never die, because there will always be someone who will want to use it, and some intellectual who will earn his keep by translating it into the fashionable language of the day.

But the most influential doctrines of Marx, though not the most dangerous, have not been those derived from his Hegelian inheritance, but from his development of the ideas of the classical economists. Above all, Marx provided for those who are attracted by the idea (which goes back to antiquity at least as

[4] The Conservative Coal Regulation Act of 1842, largely the result of Shaftesbury's work, stopped the employment of women and boys under ten. It was bitterly opposed by the Liberals, especially Bright. Similarly, the Conservatives' Ten Hours Act of 1847 had to overcome relentless opposition from Cobden and Bright. See Charles Bellairs, *Conservative Social and Industrial Reform* (London 1977).
[5] Plato, *Res Publica*, ed. J. Burnet (Oxford 1968), 338c ff.

far as Democritus and the atomists) of society as merely the reflection of underlying hidden forces, a justification for the expression of generous instincts about the clear evil of extreme poverty amongst extreme wealth. Liberal theory (at the very best, and only in some cases) said that in the end such poverty would automatically disappear; more usually it linked poverty with the failure of the poor to look after themselves. But Marx, using Ricardo's language, could provide an answer which appealed to the search for mechanistic explanations and also offered hope for the future. Certainly, he said, with Ricardo, the value of goods produced is the cost of the labour included in them. However, the value of goods should be only the cost of the direct labour; rent to the landlord and profits to the capital do not represent returns to different kinds of labour, stored in savings or invested in land; they represent merely ransoms paid to a class who, by historical circumstances have got their hands on the land and the cash. What they get—their surplus—is simply subtracted from what is rightfully the workers', since it is only the work done directly which provides the goods with any value at all. Thus capitalism is exploitation, made possible by the use of force in the past, and maintained by the present control by capitalists of the state's monopoly of force enshrined in Liberal political theory.

Once in the mood to understand the argument—and having read as one needs to read, its early ninteenth-century predecessors—it is rather satisfying. Perhaps the logical ideas of Parmenides have a similar charm for modern logicians, or the aesthetic propositions of Horace Walpole for historians of art. Having revitalised a remote intellectual world, where most of the categories of thought are alien, and whose long forgotten disputes about lost facts need an act of imagination to be comprehensible, one is inclined to say that amongst the long-dead theories this is quite an attractive ghost. It is hard now quite to remember why, for example, the labour theory of value seemed so attractive when the constant alteration of relative value amongst a far greater range of goods than Ricardo or Marx could ever have dreamt of seems to make it obvious that demand, and demand only, assigns monetary value to items bought and sold : a Palmer or a Constable forged with as much labour as Palmer or Constable originally painted is worthless;

populations used to rice may die treating the strangers' corn as valueless; the value of skills once highly sought may disappear with the invention of, say, electronic typesetting.

But it is not the ephemeral economics which the Tory fears in Marxism; he can trust rival professors to savage Marx's challenge to other, rival, certainties. It is, once again, the provision of intellectual respectability to the attack by one group in society on all other groups which is dangerous, and the invention of an argument which allows this group respectably to assault the concept of law, which it describes as being merely the notice-board laying down the rules convenient to the capitalist *status quo*. What is more, by elevating the simple categories of the classical economists—labour, capital, rent, profit—into the inevitably conflicting warriors in a historical battle from which labour will one day emerge victorious, Marx gave a fatal impetus to the concept that classes, not people, are of interest. This reinforced the tendency towards inhumanity anyway inherent in the concept of historical inevitability.

Marx's objective, his end state—communism—is a mirage which is meaningless where it is comprehensible. (What, for example, does 'to each according to his needs, from each according to his capacity' mean in the world where the State has withered and tensions between producer, society and means of production have disappeared? Who says what a need is, and who a capacity? These must be concepts, according to Marx's own theory, derived from our consciousness in the transitional period on the way to the end state.)

Marx's argument is seen at its most rickety in the *Communist Manifesto*[6] where, for example, after a splendid moralising attack on the bourgeoisie for, amongst other things, seducing each other's wives (p. 56), we are told that all the old concepts of morality derive from class antagonisms of the past; in the Communistic world both class and moral concepts as we know them will be no more, (p. 58–9). Unfortunately, in that case we do not know whether the Communist will find all this dreadful behaviour by the bourgeoisie objectionable or not. And Hegel[7] raises the common-sense problem of *needs* versus *fairness*: 'In a society based on common ownership of goods, in which provision

[6] Marx, *Communist Manifesto*, Foreign Languages Press, Peking, 1975.
[7] Hegel, *Phenomenology of Spirit*, Op. cit. p. 258.

would be made in accordance with a universal fixed rule, either each receives as much as he *needs*—in which case there is a contradiction between this inequality and the essential nature of that consciousness whose principle is the equality of individuals —or, in accordance with that principle, goods will be *equally* distributed, and in this case the share is not related to the need, although such a relationship alone constitutes the very notion of sharing'. One sometimes feels that Marx pulled off the remarkable double of getting hold of the undesirable bits of *both* Ricardo *and* Hegel.

His analysis of the historically determined progress towards the end state, offered by his attempt to put socialism on a 'scientific' basis, is full of logical nonsense and based on a mechanistic view of science which no one now believes. His recommendations for action lead to tyranny, torture, poverty and war. His theory would have died the death long since, if it had not provided the same sort of justification for powerful interests to do what they would anyway have attempted to do as has, from time to time, been offered by militant Christianity or the Jehad.

Powerful interests dressing themselves up with intellectual claptrap[8] to justify doing what they would anyway have done : in truth, the Tory was faced here with the same phenomenon which made the new capitalists Liberals. The calmest of Conservative thinkers, like Lord Hugh Cecil, saw this, and saw the extent to which the truth about the conditions of labour must be recognised, *and* the extent to which free trade should be used to counter the socialist belief that total government, by those understanding socialist truths, was a step towards the inevitable and desirable proletarian state. Others were not so calm, and the capitalists flocked to the Tory standard—as a surer defence in the coming class war with labour whose values the capitalists believed had fatally infected the Liberal Party's commitment to private property as a result of that Party's flirtation with the Radicals. Thus did the Conservative Party inherit the intellectual

---

[8] It is the Marx who wanted to have political effect, the Marx who, therefore, simplified and vulgarised his own often perceptive ideas for propaganda, the Marx who entails Lenin as Lenin entails Stalin, who is the enemy. There is much which is good, too, particularly in the young Marx. But I do not think that it is unfair to attack Marx for the way in which his ideas have been vulgarised, since he and Engels started the process themselves—above all in the *Communist Manifesto* of 1872.

tradition of their opponents—and no harm in that. The Conservative Party, still led by those who understood the sceptical Tory view of theoretical social certainties, could welcome those who, like themselves, believed in law, in property, and in the value of the individual (though the Tory might find himself alarmed by Liberal certainties even in these fields). But the Tory had carefully to keep his distance, and maintain his own instinctive knowledge. For the Liberals did not, and do not, have the whole truth any more than do the Marxists. And because we seem to be in some danger of forgetting that, we must look next at the modern form of what Lord Hailsham called in 1947 'the Liberal heresy'.

CHAPTER FIVE

Liberalism

1. Half a Philosophy.

Liberalism is very nearly true. The Conservative, we have argued, will not commit himself to *any* over-arching theory, on the grounds that all theories involve selecting which facts are to be considered important, and that all theories therefore involve the certainty of the existence of some fact which cannot be reconciled with the theory. In politics, such recalcitrant facts tend very often to be embodied in recalcitrant people: the tendency of political over-arching theory is to eliminate such people to preserve the theory. This danger, to which four-fifths of the world's population are in one way or another subject, is one reason why Conservatives fear over-arching theory since, they say, killing people because of theories is wrong—a statement which they do not derive from any system, but from their understanding of the meaning of the word 'wrong'.

Liberalism *is* an over-arching theory—but it is a unique one. It is a system which entails the permission to dissent and still be a member of the system. This can be very irritating, and Herbert Marcuse wrote a whole essay[1] expressing his irritation with the fact that the more he opposed Liberalism, the more he appeared to be behaving like a Liberal exercising his right to dissent.

But its capacity to irritate Marcuse makes Liberalism much the most congenial of ideologies to a Conservative. Liberals do not quite reach the point of agreeing that no system is permanently true—but at least they provide a rationale for not shooting people who disagree with Adam Smith and Jeremy Bentham, and this is a very unusual kind of rationale for a political theory to allow.

---

[1] Herbert Marcuse, *Repressive Tolerance,* (Beacon Press, Boston 1965).

C*

What is more, Liberalism in its classical form provides a sensible account of one way of organising part of a tolerable society. This is because the rules of economic and social behaviour on which the Liberal system is based are empirical—derived from observation—and not mystical, result of a revelation of the inevitable course which the future will take (or such like mumbo jumbo), as are those of the Marxists.

Thus what Smith and Ricardo describe when they describe an economy is something based on observation. 'If', they say, 'people behave in various ways, which is, we claim, how they do behave, these will be the consequences; and if they regularly behave in the same way, we will be able to predict the consequences'. The best Liberal writers were acute observers of reality, which is what makes Smith in particular such a delight to read. But they were observing, from the end of the eighteenth century to the early decades of this, a society which did, as the result of various happy coincidences, work rather well—and the rules they derived from watching people who lived in a fairly good society are therefore often commonsensical and practical for most situations we know.

The trouble comes in the fact that more is claimed for these rules than that they are useful rules of thumb for predicting the behaviour of a certain kind of people who have certain kinds of beliefs, or that they are guides to one kind of behaviour and motivation out of many. It is said, on the contrary, that if only those rules were followed, or allowed to work, or the institutions which protect them were rebuilt, the whole smoothly-working society from which they were derived could be restored. Thus : abolish Trade Unions, restore industrially competitive wage-bargaining, and the real wages of workers will accelerate, because a free labour market will allow a much greater efficiency of industrial output. But this ignores the vital point that it is the psychology of the day—the beliefs, morality, myths, knowledge of the day—which comes *first*. It may well have been true in a world which owned traditional beliefs about deference to authority, often in religious guise, and where a solidly-based morality of individual responsibility could be taken as so sure a datum that you hardly commented on it, that you could safely predict the behaviour of an individual worker or employer. Both would seek individual betterment within limits set by a Christian

culture pre-existing the Liberal economy, and if these limits
held, all might be well. But the Trades Union member believes
in his morality of solidarity, at least as fervently as in anything
else, and in a morality of deference to State authority not at all.
If you want to predict what he will do, you have to watch him :
he may not seek individual betterment at all—or he may not
do so in a way which is compatible with the Liberal economy.

2. *Pre-Existing Order*

It is not that the Liberal *approach* is wrong, namely to observe
facts and try to devise rules of thumb, but that having once
observed a society where pre-existing disciplines allowed very
great freedom to be given to the individual in the fair belief that
the disciplines would hold the resulting society in tolerable order,
they thought they had found a universal truth : allow maximum
freedom, and the result will be tolerable order. They tried to
build their rules of thumb into a system, and to reduce all kinds
of explanations of how people behave into the language of their
system.[2] If we look around us today, such a theory becomes as
unconvincing as any offered by the Marxists—unless the Liberal
will say what moral disciplines must be imposed on the individual to make his self-regulating mechanism work. And this,
without abandoning his trust in individual preferences, he cannot do. Hayek's 'spontaneous order'—sprung from a million
individual choices harmonising naturally into an 'organic whole'
—is in fact not spontaneous, where it occurs, at all; it derives,
in those pleasant instances, from the fact that the millions of
people concerned share enough in the way of beliefs to sort out
their conflicts peacefully.

The fact remains, however, that a good many of the rules of

---

[2] Liberal economics is at its most convincing when it is nearest to economic
journalism, describing how people often behave in their economic lives, as
the sports pages describe how they behave at other times. Liberalism is at
its least convincing when it attempts to construct an all-embracing moral
system, like that of John Stuart Mill in his 'Liberty' and Utilitarianism'.
His attempt to reduce all human motivation to a calculus of 'desires' or
'utility' avoids obvious conflict with reality only when the object of desire
or the measurement of utility is so widely defined as to make the argument
circular. The truth is, action only follows calculation of measurable benefits,
of the kind with which economics or utilitarian ethics is concerned, in quite
a small proportion of our lives.

thumb Liberals derive from observation are useful—above all, the description of usual economic behaviour which has become dignified with the title 'market theory'. What is more, certain of the defences which a good Liberal system erects to allow internal dissent (which it must allow since the individual's freedom is claimed as paramount) can usefully be taken over by Conservatives to protect those who wish to dissent from final adherence to any system—including the Liberal. To some of these institutional and constitutional protections for the dissenter or the sceptic we will return.

3. *Liberalism and Morality.*

Thus in spite of the heroic efforts of the new liberals—of whom the American Robert Nozick[3] is the most stimulating and the most brilliant—to derive moral values, or natural rights, or other unshakeable values—from a system which lacks them in the first place; despite the magnificent structure erected by the older American John Rawls[4] to provide us with a simple test whereby we may judge whether a society is just or not ('would you choose to live in it if you did not know what station you would occupy in it?'); despite the splendid writing of that veteran of many battles, the Viennese Friedrich von Hayek,[5] crying that if the rules are right, what follows *is* justice[6]—despite all this, the Liberal case rests on a fallacy. The fallacy is that the Liberal system must rest on moral foundations, and on institutions designed to preserve those foundations, which cannot be derived from it if it is to be other than mere anarchy; while at the same time the system extolls the individual in such a way that he is bound to feel free to undermine those foundations and those institutions. Nineteenth century economic Liberalism rested on the coercion implicit in Empire, on the deep rooted disciplines left over from

[3] Op. cit.
[4] and [5] See bibliography. Rawls's imposing system is vitiated by the impossibility of imagining a neutral 'original position' from which to compare the alternative societies. As Nagel puts it in the article cited in the bibliography, 'It is one of those cases in which there is no neutrality to be had, because neutrality needs as much justification as any other position.'
[6] " 'Once the rockets are up, who cares where they come down: that's not my department' says Wernher Von Braun." Tom Lehrer, 'That was the Year that Was' (Pye Records, London, 1965).

pre-industrial society—much of which actual society continued (and even now continues in a few places) alongside the industrial revolution and provided a source of moral certainty for it. It rested too on one of the toughest penal codes any society anywhere has ever seen, and on the capacity of decidedly pre-industrial, non-Liberal, local big-whigs to call out the militia if the Liberal society seemed to be challenged. For what, apart from his support for free trade, do we remember Gladstone if not his incessant moralising and his willingness to use imperial force against lesser breeds, not yet enlightened by the Liberal gospel?

4. *The Liberal Party.*

Of the Liberal Party of today, there is little that can be said since it is difficult to imagine what there can be in common between a former Labour Party city boss like Mr Cyril Smith, a dilettante restaurateur like Mr Clement Freud, and an austere son of the manse like Mr David Steel. No one would doubt that between them they add to the gaiety of nations, and sometimes (most notably in the shape of Mr Jo Grimond) perform an important function as the grit in the machine of the two-party system, preserving an honourable independent voice, which, on occasion, has said things which no one else finds it expedient to say. But coherent Liberal philosophy? Certainly not Liberal, when compulsory permanent incomes-policy is the main plank. Certainly not coherent, when an analysis of election addresses shows as wide a divergence between Liberal Party platforms in different parts of the country as between the Labour and Conservative parties. It is not the Liberal Party which has kept Liberalism alive, but those in the Conservative Party who have fought a thankless battle on its behalf like Mr John Biffen and Mr Nicholas Ridley and, once, Mr Enoch Powell—and, perhaps even more, those independent commentators like Mr Samuel Brittan, Mr Patrick Hutber, and the stalwarts of the Institute for Economic Affairs,[7] who have to put up, from the politically illiterate, with the constant accusation that they belong to the

---

[7] Above all, Arthur Selden and Ralph Harris. For a useful summary and bibliography of the contribution of the I.E.A., see their *Not from Benevolence . . . Twenty Years of Economic Dissent*, Hobart Paperbacks No. 10, (London 1977), edited by Selden and Harris.

extreme right wing, as the price for keeping alive a philosophy historically one of Conservatism's most consistent opponents.

But as for the Liberal Party, it is difficult to say what role it might have in the next few years. It depends what personalities it collects. If demoralised Social Democrats or growth-theory Conservatives joined them, they might flower briefly in the House again : but it would be a matter of transfusing blood from corpses.

5. *Liberalism and the Future*

So, true Liberalism should be seen as an argument for return to a golden age, extolling as an ideal what was in fact only one part of the way in which one quite efficient society once worked. In a world of nationalised industries, universal union membership, external trade war; a world with little freedom of movement of labour, no major transferability of land between nations; shortages, pressure-groups, media demagogues and moral anarchy; liberals will have little to say except that if it all went away things would be better. That is not to say, however, that some of the regularities of behaviour which are enshrined in liberal economics should not be taken and used as what they are : sensible rules of thumb given most (not all) human behaviour. Thus, if it has the chance, capital *will* go where it can earn a return; on the whole, people *will* respond to payments for doing things and in particular can be bribed to move from place to place or job to job with much less unpleasantness than they can be forced to do so; in short, the complex of judgements about how most people will choose, given the chance, described as the theory of the market, is a better guide to a wide area of normal, if humdrum, human behaviour than are the deeper insights of Karl Marx or the Book of Isaiah. Any politician, trying to estimate the consequences of subsidising Upper Clyde Shipbuilders or British Leyland, will need to take account of what market-theory tells him will be the consequences. But market-theory will not tell the whole story, and sometimes will only tell him trivial things : he may also have to judge what people will do, believing what they believe; what communities will live or die, and what value to put on them; what strains he is putting on the underlying moral discipline which liberal economics takes for granted. In short, he must treat market theory for what it is—a useful collection of rules of thumb—and never for what it claims to be—an over-arching theory, which will describe society as completely as simple people (but not Newton[8]) once thought Newtonian mechanics described the physical world. To get nearer to the whole truth he will need Marx and Isaiah as well —and even then the story will not be complete.

6. *Liberals and Incomes Policy*

The recent event, more than any other, which appeared to vindicate the liberal approach to economic questions was the fall of Mr Heath's Conservative government in March 1974, at a general election precipitated by the National Union of Mine-workers' failure to behave as their leaders had claimed to believe they would, and fall in behind the rest of the Trades Union movement in support of phase 3 of the then statutory incomes-policy. The refusal of the mineworkers to obey the law led to the attempt by the government to demonstrate to them, via a general election, that it was the general will of the country that they should obey, in particular because the incomes policy con-tained a mechanism (the Relativities Board) designed to meet just the kind of grievances which excited them. In addition, and perhaps confusingly, the Conservative Government called for a new mandate to impose austerity measures made necessary— and never taken until too late by the subsequent Labour Govern-ment—by the increase not only in the price of oil but also in other commodities, such as cereals and many metals, in 1972–4. For whatever reason—hiccups in the campaign, the overwhelm-ing consensus of the opinion polls that the Conservatives would win, dissatisfaction with rising prices (rising at a fraction of the rate to which the Conservative defeat inevitably led)—the Con-servatives just lost (winning more votes than Labour) in spite of the fact that the polls continued to show clear evidence that most people favoured the Government rather than the miners,

[8] 'I do not know what I may appear to the world, but to myself I seem to have been only a boy playing on the sea-shore, and diverting myself in now and then finding a smoother pebble or a prettier shell than ordinary, whilst the great ocean of truth lay all undiscovered before me.' Quoted in Brewster, *Memoirs of Newton*, Brewster, 2 vols. (London 1855), vol. 2, Chapter 27.

and believed that Conservatives rather than Labour would deal better with the worsening overseas crisis. All that was shown in reality was—as the Liberal Party learnt in 1910—how difficult it is to fight an election on a single issue; you may win for a week on your chosen issue, and then you face a downhill slide in the remaining two weeks of the campaign.[9]

But of course, there did run through the campaign one extremely dangerous and damaging question for the Conservatives, which must have contributed to that abstention by many of those who had voted for them in 1970, whose abstention lost the Conservatives the election,[10] namely, 'What if Mr Heath wins, and the miners refuse to go back? What then?'

This question, in its different forms, has really dominated political debate ever since. How can unions, or other large groups which can enforce solidarity, be compelled to obey laws for which they do not care, except by force, which is not acceptable or, probably, possible in a free society?

Much that is sensible has been learnt from the experience with the NUM. First, it has become clear that the use of the law to lead opinion, or as one of the weapons of persuasion open to government, must be treated with much more suspicion than has been fashionable since the war. If you pass a law which outlaws racial discrimination, or the possession for private use of small quantities of easily obtainable drugs, or various forms of private sexual behaviour, you will be passing a law which you cannot enforce. In a few cases (as, probably a hundred years ago with homosexuality, or today with race) a society may still wish to take this risk of unenforceability

[9] The same problem faces the proponents of the use of a referendum in such circumstances: since a referendum would be likely to be seen as a vote of confidence in the Government which called it, all sorts of issues other than those in the question would be involved. And how do you draft a question asking the electorate to choose between one highly complex negotiating package, which the union has refused, and another which it is believed it should accept? You could ask the electorate to support specific measures designed to *break* the strike, but I am not sure that that is what is envisaged. There is a place for the referendum in settling constitutional issues and, I believe, in local affairs (see page 142 below); but not in wage disputes which are bedevilled by head-counting already. What is needed in the latter are the skills of Walter Monckton, not of the political rhetorician.

[10] The increase in the Liberal vote, oddly enough, had little effect on the way constituencies changed hands.

because it wants to express in the strongest possible terms, namely with all the panoply of the law, its disgust about something. But such exhortatory laws must be few and far between if they are not to bring all law into disrepute; if such a law does not represent any particular consensus of overwhelming moral outrage (as laws about homosexuality had ceased to do by the 1960s) it is always better to err on the side of having no law and no hopeless task of enforcement for the police.

It has become clear that the use of the law to lead opinion in an effort to keep pay to sensible levels falls into the category of the unenforceable and dangerous; no consensus about the general platitude that pay should be sensibly limited will stand up against the impassioned argument for the inevitable special case to the extent of approving enforcement; breaches are spectacular, cannot be ignored and therefore damage the whole fabric of the law. To mean anything, the law has either to enter into such detail about figures and percentages as to be hopelessly unwieldy, or delegate such sweeping powers to bodies of experts as to raise serious questions about the accountability of these boards, panels and tribunals.

Thus, there were common-sense lessons to be learnt from the experiences of the winter of 1974 about the management of incomes policy and, in particular, the entrapment of a government in its own ill-judged laws.

But that was not the lesson which was drawn by Liberals, and which removed the Institute for Economic Affairs and others from the outer darkness of heresy to the centre of a new-found establishment. Their lesson was that incomes leadership, policy, or consultation was, *per se*, pernicious since it sabotaged the free market for labour, introduced impossible questions about the relative absolute worth of different occupations, politicised every wage-negotiation, demoralised management who had nothing to bargain about, and advanced us all rapidly towards a corporate state in which Trades Unions and employers would be simply agents of government, or *vice versa*, and the individual, selling his skills as best he can, would be suppressed.

7. *Conservatives and the Necessity of Incomes Leadership*

The answer to all these charges is 'Yes, but . . .'.[11] Indeed, a tight incomes-policy *does* hinder the movement of labour and the rewarding of skills—but not nearly as much as do Trades Unions and an incompetent housing policy which has made it virtually impossible to rent property. Certainly, a complete system of job-evaluation *would* involve impossible comparative decisions about the relative social worth of economics dons and dustmen, and in broad terms it is better to leave such questions to the market—but it is flying in the face of reality to believe that along with what is necessary to get people to do the job, there is not in virtually every pay-scale some element of social esteem or prize-giving already : the proof is that, in general, nicer jobs are also more highly paid. University professorships, senior journalistic posts and permanent under-secretaryships, fascinating and delightful jobs compared with most, should be virtually unpaid in a Liberal world; that they are in fact well rewarded is not wrong, but the result of the fact that we do really accept some element of their pay as being a badge of status and a support for hierarchy.

Certainly incomes policy, particularly statutory incomes policy, introduces politics into wage negotiations and puts the government behind management who are trying to stick to the limits—but when half our trades unions have statutes which commit them (like the National Union of Mineworkers) to the destruction of capitalism and the imposition of socialism, does not politics enter into it already? And do the commentators honestly believe that the incomes policy of 1975–77 has not helped serious management to keep wages within reasonable bounds?

And, certainly, most important of all, there *are* real dangers of the political theory of the corporate state coming to be accepted as the only practical system for the running of a modern nation. According to such a theory, people only count as mem-

[11] The fact that the Conservative, possessor of no simple system which provides him with a ready answer to every question, has to spend so much time saying, 'Yes, but . . .' puts him at a disadvantage in terms of today's demagogy. To be the Robespierre of the television age, you do not need an ability to make three hour speeches, but to give ninety second long answers to tendentious questions from news reporters. Answers beginning 'Yes, but . . .' do not do at all. That is why the Conservative cause needs the services of real genius to get its more subtle case across, genius which we lack at present. See also p. 75, below.

bers of the productive organisations to which they belong, are
represented only through it, and disciplined only by it, and the
State becomes the creature of the corporations (as some might
say it still is in Japan). This particular over-arching theory—it
is properly called Fascism—is due to be back in vogue soon,
starting, as is usually the case with extreme political views,
amongst the students and dons, disillusioned socialists, and
extreme nationalists.

All these dangers are real. All are worse, the tighter and more
detailed the incomes policy is, and are most compellingly adduced
against a statutory policy. They are the Scylla on one side of a
government's course. But the Charybdis is real too. Let us remind
ourselves why intelligent men, well understanding these real dangers, have again and again sought out a path of government-led
incomes policy, and why they will, and must, continue to do so.

8. *Incomes Policy and the Future: Why Liberalism is Dangerous for the Conservative Party.*

Let us cast our mind back to the 1970 Conservative Manifesto,
an efficient document which did its job well. It contained, however, in one glaring internal contradiction the seeds of the ensuing disputes in the Conservative Party. First, on page six, is the
resounding declaration: 'We utterly reject the philosophy of
compulsory wage control.' Then, on page fourteen comes, 'We
will progressively reduce the involvement of the State in the
nationalised industries. . . . So as to improve their competitive-
ness.' But then, on pages eleven to twelve, is found the justification for the massive intervention in the pay and prices of public
industry which was in fact the rule between 1970 and 1974:
'The first essential is for the new Government to give a new
lead. We will subject all proposed price rises in the public sector
to the most searching scrutiny. If they are not justified, they will
not be allowed. In implementing our policies, we will give overriding priority to bringing the present inflation under control.'[12]
Price control means concern with costs. Cost control includes wage

12 Even in the language of Manifestos, more highly coloured than clearly
defined, the contradiction between a policy of non-intervention and no
incomes policy and a policy of direct action, initially on the prices (and
therefore the wages) of nationalised industries, is stark. One approach or
the other had to give way, and in fact, of course, it was the first.

control. Public sector wage control led inevitably to private sector wage control. To put it another way, if the Government, treated as the employer, whatever the nationalised industry statutes say,[13] is not to sabotage the labour market and much else by being a profligate payer of its own people, it must have a view as to what they should be paid. Few, if any, of the larger nationalised industries can be dressed up convincingly as businesses with competitors whose costs they must match since they have usually been nationalised just *because* they hold a monopoly of some natural resource or service and *have* no competitors. Others are, or should be, without any pretence social services, like railways, hospitals, or posts, which can never now pay if their coverage is to be universal. Therefore, across a great range of Government employment, the judgement of what pay increases should be allowed is related to no sanction of the form 'if we pay you that, we will go bust as a company' but only to one of the form 'if we pay you that we will go bust as a country'. It is the judgement of what this level is, and its enforcement over the public sector, which lies at the heart of every incomes policy.

What happened in 1971–2, after a period of initial success with a policy of bringing down the rate of pay increases in nationalised industries—involving the breaking of almost the only public-sector strike which can easily be broken, that by the unfortunate postmen—was that public-sector settlements became lower than they were in the private sector. Reasonably enough, public sector trades unionists, fired with mounting anger amongst their members—demonstrated in the first miners' dispute and in the electricity workers' go-slow—argued that they would only tolerate wage restraint if it was even-handed; that is, if it applied also to the private sector. Hence the overall freeze; hence, because of the well-understood problems of an explosion of frustrated claims at the end of a freeze, the attempt gradually to relax the statutory controls via stages two and three. Statutory controls? Yes—not because Mr Heath's cabinet were suddenly converted to a belief in the corporate state, but for the very opposite reason : a statutory policy, it was argued, was less corporatist than a so-

[13] In fact, when the post-war corporations were set up, under the influence of Herbert Morrison in particular, such a to-do was made about how nationalisation now gave the State the opportunity to set an example in all sorts of areas of industrial practice, that workers can hardly be blamed for thinking that they are to all intents and purposes State employees.

called voluntary policy which was enforced by union bosses acting as the non-accountable agents of Government—since a statutory policy left responsibility with Parliament. These are real
arguments, real questions. The last argument (in favour of the
statutory version) is wrong—there is in effect no difference in
terms of corporate statism between a voluntary policy enforced
by union leaders and a law only obeyed because union leaders
say it should be obeyed, and much more danger to the fabric of
law in the statutory version. But it is nonetheless a respectable
argument and was genuinely held. That the former argument,
about the control of public sector wages, is real, is proved by the
way it has confronted every British Government of recent time,
including, of course, Labour Governments between 1964 and
1970, and after 1974.

9. *The Need for a Philosophy of Government.*
Great harm will be done by the false expectations aroused by
simple monetarists who claim that control of the money supply
avoids these questions. Many Liberals, including Hayek, are
wiser, and understand that the real question is who is to control
those parts of the system which force the money supply to be
increased, notably public-sector Trades Unions. Hayek, after
all, supported Conservative attempts to limit Trades Union privileges by law in 1971. The next Conservative Government will
be right not to go naked into office, armed only with the anti-
governmental philosophy of Liberalism, to deal with these questions of power and control. If it were to do that it would find itself
forced by reality to cobble together what philosophy of government it could under the stress of crisis, and it would be too late.

Economic Liberalism is a splendid philosophy for opposition,
as is anarchism or extreme socialism, since it enables you to support all the pressure groups who are resisting the government of
the day, and to say that they are fine Liberal fellows downtrodden
by the arrogance of bureaucratic government. This is why the
Conservative Party always becomes more Liberal[14] in opposition
and why the Labour Party becomes more anarchistically socialist.

[14] This is normally described by journalists who have got in a muddle about
their terminology and should all read Sam Brittan's *Left or Right—the
Bogus Dilemma*, (London 1968), once a year as therapy, as becoming more
right wing.

It is not only because of activists in the constituencies: there are plenty of proper Tory activists who are not Liberals. In power, both parties swing back, not towards some 'centre' on a continuum from left to right which does not exist, but towards the necessity of finding some philosophy which enables them to resist excessive wage claims in the public sector and, in general, effectively to use the authority of the State. Future Labour governments are likely to find such a philosophy in Marxism which will justify control in the interests of the proletarian future rather than in 'moderatism'. Future Conservative administrations are better equipped—with the Tory tradition of the role of the State as arbiter amongst the different communities and individuals of the nation—and should not worry themselves into a neurosis about abandoning Liberalism in office. They owe no debt to Liberalism, even if there are some battles they can fight alongside their nineteenth-century opponents.

CHAPTER SIX

A Conservative–Liberal Common Cause: The Separation of Powers

The aspect of Liberalism most interesting to a Conservative is its constitutional theory designed to preserve the capacity to dissent. Conservatives value it from fundamental scepticism about the possibility of determining final truth in this world; Liberals because they think that competition of ideas generates an order which amounts to final truth. In practical political terms, they can often be allies, as is shown by the history of the modern Conservative Party. In the next chapter we discuss one area of agreement—the Constitution.

1. Separation of Powers

Conservatives know that ultimately the State must be supreme because, human nature being what it is, if there are equal powers in the land, civil war will eventually obtain. But Conservatives, like Liberals, should greatly fear the present tyranny of the House of Commons. Unchecked, in other than trivial senses, by the House of Lords or the Monarch; dominating the courts and the traditions of common law with an ever-increasing volume of statute-law and an ever increasing number of special administrative tribunals from which appeal lies to a Minister and not to a court; brandishing the theory of the detailed mandate in the face of reasoned argument, the legal power of a majority in the British House of Commons has increased, is increasing and ought to be diminished.

In reality, of course, such power is limited by the fact that a democratically elected body is much averse to enforcing anything, at least against anyone who can make a fuss and cause Ministerial unpopularity; but the fact remains that the power of the House of Commons to revolutionise statute law, to debauch the currency, to overturn ancient rights or duties, to manufacture new rights and duties, is unlimited, except perhaps in so far as it is bound by treaty obligations, including the Treaty of Rome. But what treaty-organisation to which we belong is going to enforce upon a recalcitrant House of Commons major-ity its obligations under treaty? Arm-twisting about support for sterling or such-like might limit irresponsible behaviour *vis-à-vis* the EEC or NATO if our general morale and our reserves were low : but as relations between France and America show, it can be the arm-twister who suffers in such encounters.

The truth is, our constitution is dangerously vulnerable to capture by the minority who can get hold of a political party which then, for one reason or another, gains a majority in the House. This state of affairs make it all too plausible that the worst nightmare of Conservative or Liberal alike—the capture of the executive by a totalitarian clique which would sub-sequently impose its intellectually disreputable certainties at the barrel of a gun—could become a reality. In the meantime, it has various perverse and unsatisfactory results. It means that political parties concentrate on, and are productive only of, legislation, because once you have a majority, legislation is the only thing that is easy. Constant legislative flux has enormous costs—to which we shall return later in our discussion of the need for the strengthening of free standing communities apart from the state. It means, paradoxically, that executive power drains *away* from backbench members of the House of Commons since the majority, once obtained, can be whipped into line on virtually any measure (excepting occasionally great issues of principle, or issues which affect MPs personally, like their pay) by its Prime Ministerial ring-master who holds the whip of a dissolution over it, and dangles fat bunches of patronage carrots in front of its nose.

The effectiveness of the whip's discipline means that executive power rests with those who have the power to initiate, not those who have the power to rubber stamp; and those who have the power to initiate action (or non-action) are Ministers; but Minis-ters are lone figures at the summits of great Departments of State : not surprisingly, the first rush of self-confidence over, Ministers become, with few exceptions, the creatures of their Departments. Thus, paradoxically, the result of a tyrannical concentration of democratic power results in the passing of power away from directly democratic hands altogether—to the Civil Service who control the executive.

Other tendencies lead to the same result. The House of Commons has few brilliant men now; some very stupid; some security risks. As a cross section of the populace, it is not bad : as a pool from which to draw Ministers who have to face civil servants, Trades Unionists and industrialists all, in different ways, selected by vigorous competition, it is hopelessly inadequate. On these no more than average people a ridiculous work load of largely pointless activity is landed : being a rubber stamp may keep you up until three in the morning for week after week; while the expectations generated by membership of a body which claims, and technically has, unlimited power, mean an ever greater burden of constituency and other lobbying on matters about which the member can in fact do little. The circle is vicious : strenuous but largely pointless work attracts few of high calibre; the lack of high calibre, publicly demonstrable, together with the members' inability to affect anything much, keeps their status low in the public eye (and their pay in line with their status); not surprisingly, then, even fewer of real quality feel tempted by the job.

Again, the growth of government and the alleged complexities of the financing of it leave a smaller and smaller area about which the average member can sensibly comment. Television, needing for its three-minute slots the modern equivalent of the crudest demagogues of antiquity, (though the modern technique is not the great oration but, on the contrary, the homely cliché) makes into ephemeral heroes just those people in the House least able substantially to influence policy.

All this has pushed power into what Hecclo and Wildavsky[1] rightly call the Whitehall village—a closed, quiet community with its own values and its own objectives. Thus our system is one where the direct exercise of power is very secret and very little accountable,[2] and is likely to remain so, unless there should come to power a party so confident and so arrogant that it would

[1] H. Hecclo and A. Wildavsky, *The Private Government of Public Money*, (London 1973).
[2] Jock Bruce-Gardyne and Nigel Lawson, in their useful book *The Politics of Power* show how patient the detective work has to be to discover even basic facts about even the greatest Government decisions.

smash the Civil Service and break wholly free; and then the danger would be a worse one, of the use by an arrogant majority of its full, constitutional, tyrannical power.[3]

Conservatives and Liberals alike then believe that the constitution is at present dangerously rickety. Four areas of reform are worth considering: reform of Westminster, reform of the voting system, reform of the relations between Westminster and Whitehall, and reform of relations between the executive and the law.

2. *The Need for a Second Chamber*

The most important object of the second chamber should be to present obstacles—not insuperable, but significant—to the House of Commons if that body should find itself temporarily in the hands of a revolutionary or radical majority. Ultimately, such a majority must have its way, and face such consequences as reality and the electorate may dictate. But it is possible at present for an administration with a majority, if it has for the time being defeated civil service opposition, or if the issue is one with which the civil service is not concerned, to be revolutionary in the most frivolous possible way. With analysis of the consequences of the most intellectually shoddy kind, governments may nationalise great industries, impose laws on Trades Unions, threaten the freedom of the press, or destroy the housing market. Fashions arise, in legislation as in anything else—for the floating of the pound, or statutory incomes policy, or the reorganisation of local government—the object may be worthy, but the plan can be carried through far too easily. This is not what it feels like to activist Ministers, of course, who complain about the one remaining check which there is, namely, the shortage of legislative time in the House of Commons. Every reforming government, Mr Heath's no less than Mr Wilson's in 1974, begins to mutter about the need for quicker procedures and more delegated legislation—as if Britain's problems stemmed from a shortage of legislation! The truth is quite the reverse. As Bacon and Eltis point out, virtually every nostrum of the macro-economic tinker-

[3] The minority report by Brian Sedgemore, MP attached to the Eleventh Report of the Expenditure Committee of the House of Commons, September, 1977, shows that there is no shortage of potential recruits for such a Government.

ers has been carried out since 1960—every fashionable new tax has been tried, every kind of shift of demand and currency management.[4] As Professor Wilson[5] argues, regional policy, pensions and other important areas have been in flux for decades. The number of pages of statute law passed every year seems to increase exponentially: and yet the likes of Mr Edward Short as Leader of the House can diagnose 'the legislative log-jam' as a problem facing government![6] The people of Britain should send to the House of Commons the message Clement Attlee once sent to Harold Laski: 'A period of silence on your part would be welcome.'[7]

But it is too much to hope that the House of Commons would maintain a self-denying ordinance over legislation. The only hope is to restore to the Upper House the capacity to make the log-jam deplored by Mr Short much worse; to allow it to delay bills for longer; to do away with the antiquated rule that the Upper House cannot touch 'money bills'; in short, to make the Upper House a formidable institution again.

Of course, this implies a change in the basis of membership of the Upper House. Only an elected body would find the self-confidence to stand against an elected Lower House. It should be elected on as different a basis as possible from the Lower House, so that a majority in the one is not rubber stamped by the same majority in the other. It should probably be elected on a different electoral basis—such as a pure proportional system—to make difficult the emergence of *any* single majority, and its members should not all come up for election at the same time. The object would be to produce something akin to a national jury to set against the initiating Lower House—indeed, the inventors of democracy, the Athenians, might well have used the lot to select

[4] Robert Bacon and Walter Eltis: *Britain's Economic Problem: Too Few Producers*, (Macmillan, London 1976) p. 5-6.
[5] In S. E. Finer, ed., *Adversary Politics and Electoral Reform*, (London 1975).
[6] *The Sunday Times*, May 25th, 1975 reported Mr Short (now Lord Glenamara) as suggesting that the process of passing new laws could be simplified by having a 'general Enabling Bill' dealing with a whole range of subjects affecting one Government department, instead of having one Act of Parliament for each subject. Asked on the BBC radio programme The Week in Westminster whether he was suggesting that Ministers might be able to act 'with blanket power', Mr Short replied, 'I think this is inevit-able—and of course this process has been going on for years.'
[7] Quoted in Joe Haines, *The Politics of Power*, (Cape, London 1977), p. 13.

a random membership for it, and thus divorce it from electoral politics entirely, while preserving its democratic credentials. Sadly, however, in a nation of fifty-five million, we must put that aside as impractical, while reminding ourselves that election is not the only, or the oldest, method of democratic selection.

Thus the powers of the Upper House need only be strengthened, not qualitatively altered; what must be provided for it is a base from which to wield its powers. The present situation, of theoretical powers, never used for fear of the abolition of the whole chamber, is absurd and dangerous.

A bonus from such a proposal, attractive to Conservatives, would be the separation of the honours system from Parliament. An honours system is a sensible way of avoiding a state of affairs where money is a society's only reward, and of honouring quiet achievement and endeavour in a way fairly well divorced from political chicanery. There is no reason why an honour should not be carried down through the generations: that his children will be honoured for his achievement is no mean incentive to a public servant. But the days of hereditary legislation have gone; an elected Upper House would restore the pleasant possibility of new hereditary honours.

Nor should we much mind the ending of the present assembly, part hereditary peers who seldom dare exercise their powers, part life-creations, many of whom seldom speak. The great men who come as life peers would still hold our attention, and that of the media, if they made their speeches elsewhere; the lesser men represent merely another example of the already excessive patronage of the Prime Minister. That an elected Upper House would end a system whereby Prime Ministers (and Leaders of the Opposition) can appoint members of Parliament would be nothing but a gain. On this latter subject Conservatives can make common cause with the former peer, Mr Anthony Wedgwood Benn.

3. *Electoral Reform*

Many distinguished scholars, such as Professors Finer and Wilson,[8] and not a few good parliamentarians, such as Lords Carr and Carrington, believe that the problems of legislative

[8] In Finer, op. cit.

flux and of the tyranny of the House of Commons stem from the system of first-past-the-post voting for that House which can enable a party to achieve a clear majority with a relatively small proportion of the votes. In October 1974, for example, Labour won a clear majority with only 28% of the possible votes; and in 1951 the Conservatives were returned though Labour won more votes.

This diagnosis, however, is confused. The fact that laws are overturned, policies abandoned and U-turns navigated is because governments change, or dominant factions within parties change; having changed, the new majority, free of checks, finds it all too easy to undo everything which went before. If the electoral reformers are saying that they can so gerrymander the vote that the government will seldom change—some (psephologically imaginary) moderate middle remaining for ever in power—then they are saying something dangerous and foolish, since the difficult trick of changing administrations without violence and constitutional disaster is one which Westminster turns much more regularly than any other Parliament. As a matter of fact, the coalition politics offered by the reformers would arguably be highly conducive to chopping and changing of policy, since negotiations amongst factions would be on the basis of deals on policy. Even now, many changes are changes within the life of one government.

The truth is, in so far as the problem is not the fundamental one of a divided and uncertain nation, running after every quack remedy offered, it is constitutional, not electoral. The solution is to leave the Lower House, with its clear majority—the product of local and comprehensible elections, not of deals between the financial backers and the party organisations of splintered factions—as the initiator; but to restore the checks and balances against frivolous initiatives.[9]

9 A further argument sometimes advanced by the reformers—and the Liberal Party—is that it is unfair that some millions of scattered Liberal votes secure less seats than, say, the regionally concentrated Scottish National Party. The answer to that is, first, that it is somewhat patronising to assume that those Liberal voters do not know what they are doing—namely voting against both the big parties without committing themselves to another group of potential Ministers; and second, that the SNP actually *represent* something—they control communities and territory, and inspire, even to excess, a real following. They have a cause and a cry. Where in Britain—except round some personality—do the Liberals do the same?

4. *Westminster and Whitehall*

Reform within the Palace of Westminster is the first and most important step towards limiting the arbitrary power of a single chamber Parliament—a power which could be used to attempt to impose tyranny, and is already used to keep the laws in a state of flux to the great detriment of that stability which (we shall argue in the next section) is necessary for the growth of natural communities within the nation, without which social life is not satisfactorily possible. We shall return in some detail to this concept of community, and how it was damaged first by industrialisation, and now by the more or less random alterations to the framework of life which result from the activities of a legislature and an executive which find social experimentation far too easy. It is that experimentation which it should be one of the functions of the constitution to limit; but ours, for long thought to be all the more effective for being unwritten, is now not only unwritten, but forgotten, except in its more mechanical aspects. Conservatives can join wholeheartedly with Liberals in the search for ways of restoring an effective constitution, and can ask with Hayek the question 'What function is served by a constitution which makes omnipotent government possible?'[10]

The effect of the absorption of total power by the House of Commons, power that can be, and therefore is, exercised almost at the whim of those who control the majority, has not yet been to impose a thoroughgoing plan of any kind on the country. So far the majorities in control have been too divided amongst themselves, too unsure of what they wanted or how to get it, to do other than tinker, experiment, reform in a piecemeal way, and overturn whatever their predecessors have done. The result externally on society, as we shall see, has been disastrous enough, and has kept Britain from the natural regeneration which might otherwise have been possible. As far as the exercise of power within the executive goes, however, the capacity of the House of Commons to approve whatever it is told by its majority leader to approve, but not to initiate other than on the rarest of occasions, has, paradoxically, as we have seen actually contributed to the growth of power outside the democratic system altogether. Since the executive need not worry about getting its

[10] F. A. von Hayek, *Law, Legislation and Liberty* Vol I (London, 1973) p. 1.

initiatives through Parliament (except on very rare occasions), it is the people who have a say about what the initiatives are who matter.

The first way, therefore, of restoring some measure of real power to Parliament, and taking it from the Ministers (really the Departments) whose initiate is, paradoxically, to limit the power of the Lower House. If the Lower House knew that, whatever the whips might say, a piece of legislation might well founder upstairs, members of that Lower House would be in a far stronger position to delay and amend legislation coming from their own party the wisdom of which they doubted: the Chief Whip bullying the recalcitrant member with the usual threats would face the reply, 'It is not going through in that form in the end anyway—and as for delay, it looks as if it will take two years of inter-house negotiation before anything is on the statute book. How can you say that the whole government intention stands or falls by every clause in the first version you have brought forward?' What is more, the most powerful possible way of directing the attention of civil servants to the fact that they should take account of the preferences of parliamentarians would be the posing by Westminster of real obstacles to the passage of Departmental legislation. At present, Westminster is regarded by civil servants as a legislative sausage-machine, with a Chief Whip whose job it is to churn out the legislative sausages made up in Whitehall. Only on very rare occasions, such as the passage of Mr Heath's European legislation or the non-passage of Mr Foot's 1976 devolution bill, does Parliament hiccup at present. It is not easy to remember an occasion, apart from Europe (and that was a pretty foregone conclusion), in the period between 1971 and 1974 when it entered the heads of anybody in Whitehall that it was worth considering what would happen to proposals in Parliament—let alone whether Parliament might have something positive to contribute to them. Doubtless the Whips worried—but they had a majority of thirty-one with which to calm their nerves.

Thus the basic answer to the problem of an over-mighty civil service is to restore Parliament as a place which, by its constitution, is likely to be the forum of real argument and to present real obstacles to the smooth output of legislative sausages generated in Departments.

5. *Secrecy.*

There are various, relatively tinkering reforms which would
sensibly increase efficiency in Whitehall and restore its con-
nections with the outside world. The most important of these,
often recommended by oppositions, never done by governments,
relates to secrecy. There are things known and said in Whitehall
which should remain very secret. There is a real area of defence
secrecy. There is a real area of commercial secrecy. There is a
small area where exact knowledge of government intentions
might enable someone to make money—though it is a far smaller
area that commonly supposed, since it is normally the knowledge
by a few of what is generally secret which is profitable; if there
was no secret in the first place, no advantageous private knowledge could exist. Most budget secrets—which are treated in
Whitehall with something approaching the security which applies
to our nuclear capability—are of this class. They are artificial
secrets: if discussion of all the options, all the forecasts, was
open, no one could make money out of it since all the markets
would have all the information. It is the leak which is dangerous, but the leak presupposes the secret. This fact is, of course,
well understood in Whitehall, where it is equally well understood that the real purpose of Budget secrecy is to protect the
Treasury's dominant position in the budgetary process, since the
fact that only the Treasury knows in full the kind of options
which are being discussed excludes participation by other Departments or outsiders.

The Government's short-term economic forecasts are another
good example of this syndrome: treated now with the utmost
secrecy, the security is only necessary because if privileged outsiders saw these sacred writings, they would have special knowledge of what the Government might do. If, however, the
Treasury forecasts were openly published, alongside any other
privately produced forecasts, they would lose their mystery and
their special significance. They could also be openly criticised
by non-government professionals—and, who knows, might even
turn out to be not the most impressive pieces of analysis ever
seen.

Finally, there should be secrets, or rather honourable trust,
between Ministers and each other and between Ministers and
their senior confidential advisers. Mr Crossman did not under-

stand that. By giving us the backstairs gossip, he did nothing to open up real areas of public concern, and much to sour relations between Ministers and advisers for many years. The inevitable result is that civil servants—justifiably using the argument that Ministers cannot be trusted to behave decently in normal working relationships—will keep even more from their masters. No organisation—business, Trades Union, school, newspaper or university—can run effectively if every member has to fear the published ésprit d'escalier of every other. As usual, in its fascination with the Crossman diaries, the British press was interested in the personalities and the froth, not the real issues.[11]

The area from which secrecy should be drawn back is the area of analysis. The facts, or supposed facts, on which policy is to be based should always be published, in advance, for scrutiny. The options and counter-options should always be open to outside scrutiny. Not only would this improve the quality of the information on which government finally acts, but it might help to generate a new breed of political commentators and policy experts in Britain, who would be in a position to match the expertise of their American counterparts. We can hardly blame the press for writing about trivia as it does now, if it is a crime for it to get the facts it needs. But it remains true, that just as Parliament hardly impinged on my Whitehall life, so also there was no single occasion which I can remember when press comment or analysis deflected a serious government policy in any significant way. It should not be possible for this to be so.

6. *Strangers in the Whitehall Village*
Amongst the other remedies and marginal improvements proposed, it would be sensible to take and develop further the system of special advisers to Ministers.

A Minister, even with his two or three juniors, is an extremely lonely figure surrounded by civil servants cleverer and more

[11] De Jouvenel, *Sovereignty*, p. 77, touches on a more fundamental reason for fearing too regular and effective a mockery of political leaders in large societies when he says, surely rightly, that 'The more distant that an authority is, the more it needs a halo, or if no halo is available, the more policemen it will need.' The argument, if true, is also a powerful plea for the return of authority to smaller units.

D

experienced than he is (in the great majority of cases), whose skills are the skills of analysis and administration. The politician has his skills, if he is any good, but some of them are not very relevant to the management of a Department. He should, therefore, be able to bring in advisers who are also friends, to be eyes and ears, and to read for him and argue for him at the different levels in the Department to which he will seldom penetrate. But if the system is to develop, it must be a little formalised to prevent abuse; the advisers should be temporary civil servants, under the same disciplines as those with whom they work (though they must leave with the Minister). They must be subject to security vetting of at least the same rigour as civil servants. The best way of organising them would be to group political special advisers, civil service private secretaries and other technical advisers, in roughly equal numbers, into something like a European 'Cabinet' under the administrative discipline of the Principal Private Secretary, a civil servant. But it must be emphasised that vital though the opening up of Whitehall's analytical process may be; useful though more outside experts with Ministers could be, the key lies in removing the predictability of the way in which Parliament wields its rubber stamp on what Whitehall devises. That done, much else will follow.

7. *The New Bill of Rights.*

Many intelligent and far-sighted Conservatives, notably Lord Hailsham,[12] have argued that one way of restoring some protection to the individual and the community against the overweening State—and to all three against the depredations of communities who refuse to look to any interests but their own (what might be called rogue communities)—would be to formulate a new Bill of Rights to augment that which is already enshrined in our law. Many Liberals too, looking to the strength and effectiveness of that great Liberal construction, the American Constitution—a constitution which effectively removed a corrupt party leader, still in control of his party, in a way which our

[12] Lord Hailsham's 1976 Dimbleby Lecture *Elective Dictatorship*, (London 1976) and Lord Justice Scarman's 1974 Hamlyn Lectures *English Law—The New Dimension* (London 1974), are essential reading on this subject.

poor unwritten affair could not conceivably have matched—have toyed with this approach.

But it is very difficult to imagine how it would come about that a new list of basic rights, which was not platitudinous, could either be drawn up or agreed. Such a settlement is normally only successful at some time of conscious national political reorganisation : after a declaration of independence, a glorious revolution or restoration, or a national revival after defeat or disaster. It is not quite inconceivable, looking at the dangers ahead of us, that some such watershed may be crossed in the years ahead. But the dangers of disaster at least equal the chances of new birth in such a process of cutting free from the past; it is not a prospect for which we can sensibly plan or on a successful resolution of which we can count. The nearest we may get to it is a watershed we have already, relatively quietly, passed : entry to the European Community. And, as Lord Justice Scarman points out,[13] the full implications of our adherence to the European Convention of Human Rights may not yet have been understood. In so far as this adherence can be used to revivify traditional rights, Conservatives and Liberals alike should welcome it, and seek to use it. More may not be possible.

[13] Op. cit.

PART III

Conservatism, Community and the Future

CHAPTER ONE

Introduction

In the last chapter we looked at some of the ways in which the individual citizen, the traditional pattern of living, the existing successful institution, might be protected against the depredations of a House of Commons whose unlimited authority has become subservient to a secret, unaccountable executive power. A suggestion or two has been made, in passing, about efficiency as well; there is no harm in making the present unsatisfactory system deliver the goods a little more regularly while we consider more fundamental changes. But we must now turn to a more difficult task. The future, it is certain, holds many dangers as well as opportunities. For the sake of argument, we offered one account of the future earlier in this book, and tried to predict some of the coming political issues. We then went on to argue the irrelevance of social democratic and Liberal philosophies to these issues; and the dangerous nonsense inherent in Marxism. What then of the horse which we wish our reader to back, the Conservative runner? What we have to do now is to show, first, the kind of paths for society which might be tolerable as a way through the minefield of the future, and, second, why the Conservative tradition, embodied in the kind of Conservative party which is likely to exist, might be a sensible guide along that path.

To do this, it is necessary to introduce the concept of 'community' to which, it will be argued, society must return in the future if life is to be tolerable, and then to show how the Conservative approach is compatible with it and how Conservative policies, in the shorter term, embody it.

CHAPTER TWO

The need for Conservative Community

1. Why Community is Fundamental.

Man and his community are inseparable. The Liberal language of individual rights, which appears to put the individual first, and is usually justified by a parable about the origin of society in which the individual precedes the community, is simply a special category of the language of community. Just as you cannot have a private language, because words derive their meaning from use, and therefore it is inevitable that language inheres in community where people to talk to one another,[1] so you cannot have private rights which no-one else acknowledges. When we talk about rights, we are talking about part of communal life. A right is in fact part of an institution for the settlement of disputes within a community, if such is needed: you only need rights where you have formal arbitration about conflicts. Where there is accepted authority, strong enough to settle disputes without argument (as perhaps in an authoritarian family), no one is concerned about rights at all. Thus a community existing happily without the concept of rights is perfectly feasible, though the happiness would rely on benevolence on the part of the supreme authority, and on the skill with which that authority settled disputes in ways acceptable to the community.

The state of nature for man is, then, community. Community is the condition of language, of reproduction and the secure bringing up of children, of worship, and of most of the best candidates for the criteria which separate men from animals. Community is also the condition of man's so far rather tenuous survival, since co-operative effort, the storage and transmission over time of practical knowledge, and the diffusion of new survival tricks, depend in the first instance on co-operation in a

[1] See the discussion of private language in Wittgenstein, *Philosophical Investigations*, Trans. Anscombe, (Oxford, Blackwell, 1958) paragraph 256 ff.

continuing community. Equally, of course, the community has no life of its own, except as a metaphor, and the origin of co-operative effort, the invention of knowledge and the capacity to experiment lie with individuals.

Without a community, an individual is in an unnatural state : Marx's discussion of alienation,[2] and Durkheim's of anomie, were the first systematic attempts to describe the results for man when he has no community. The former analysed the effects of increasing conflict between man and the unnatural social and economic world of the early industrial revolution; the latter correlated the decline of effective community with, among other things, suicide-rates.[3] Many others have followed. But it is not only as a condition for individual happiness that community is essential. If those theorists of scientific method[4] who argue that advance in science (on which, presumably, depends our capacity in the longest term to survive as a race at all) derives from shifts in the locus of interest, or the criteria for importance among the scientific community, then even in that area (traditionally one preserve where the solitary genius was thought by laymen to come into his own) progress depends crucially on the inter-action of community and individual. Even scientific progress is found not to be a comprehensible concept in terms of the individual alone; the community and its needs define what is accepted as progress.

The definition of man as man apart from animals; happiness and survival : all are dependent on the survival of community. Obviously, communities in which there is abuse of power, as Leach[5] argues there is in the modern small family, can become engines of destruction for the individual, and then for them-selves. But in such a situation the need is for new communities, not for the freeing of individuals as independent atoms.

[2] E.g. Karl Marx, 1844 Manuscripts, p. 134 ff in *Marx, The Early Texts*, ed. D. McLellan, and *Capital*, Vol. I, p. 165 ff, (Penguin, London 1976).
[3] E. Durkheim, *Suicide, a Study in sociology*. Trans. J. A. Spaulding and G. Simpson, (London, 1952).
[4] See for example, T. S. Kühn, *Logic of Discovery or Psychology of Research?* in *Criticism and the Growth of Knowledge*, ed. Imre Lakatos and Alan Musgrave, Cambridge University Press, 1970. The contribution of Lakatos himself to this excellent symposium discusses the issues clearly.
[5] Sir Edmund Leach, *A Runaway World?* 1967 Reith Lectures, (London, 1968). Leach rightly points out the historical oddity of today's tiny, isolated families. A proper community should provide relief from this claustrophobia, with the help of relations, co-workers, neighbours and friends.

D*

These are the values—the values of community—which are threatened by the destabilising effect of an ever-increasing government and an ever more fluid society. A community needs its landmarks, social or physical, around which to group; if these change more rapidly than the members of the community can adapt, the community will fall to pieces or develop into an aggressive pressure group for its own protection—what may be called a rogue community. The encroachment of government, borne along by the trends we have noted, is destroying the capacity for other than defensive, or potentially rogue, communities in Britain.

2. *Nation, State and Communities*

Before going further, it may help to define some terms. By '*nation*' is meant a political entity (such as the United Kingdom of Great Britain and Northern Ireland—a relatively recent creation (1921) in its present shape). '*State*' will be used to refer to the political institutions which control a nation (in our case, those under the direct or delegated control of the Queen in Parliament). '*Community*'—our central concept—will be used to refer to cohesive social groups which, we argue, are the natural building blocks of . . . '*society*' by which we mean whatever communities and individual people live within the political boundaries of the nation. Thus: 'the nation can only exist if the State holds sway over all the communities and individuals of society', would be, by our definitions, a sentence which meant something, though the truth of the proposition it expresses would be controversial.

Many things go into the delineation of a nation and since its defining characteristic is, literally, an act of drawing lines, many of the relevant factors are to be found in political and diplomatic history. Acts of Union, secession, conquests and defeats, political marriages, may all create or alter nations; they need have no effects on the society within the newly-drawn boundaries except perhaps to alter the institutions of the State. Most nations come into being by a honeycomb-process of the aggregation of cohesive communities, usually under the original aegis of one particularly strong community. What differentiates a nation as a nation, and not a province of an empire, is a difficult question which seems to rest on what its governors feel : if they feel that they rule a State independent of all others, they probably do, whatever treaties they have signed. Thus the members of the present European Community clearly remain independent nations, though they have legally passed considerable power to a supranational centre; on the other hand East Germany, though technically quite independent, for reasons of ideology and military domination is doubtfully so. Obviously the confidence of the state in its independence will rest largely on the assessment the governors make of their actual freedom to do what they like regardless of outside pressures. The progress from a wholly independent nation to a mere province is a continuum, and different states will feel themselves to have lost their freedom of action at different points along the line. That is why the use of the word 'sovereignty' is to be avoided where possible since it injects a clarity of distinction not found in the real world.

Clearly, still, the United Kingdom is a nation and a nation which has existed in something like its present form for so long that it came at one time near to turning itself altogether into one national community. It is the bonds that gather people into communities which are the primary organising forces in society. A nation will fall apart if the communities within it decide to re-write political boundaries, unless other communities are willing, and strong enough, to compel adherence to the *status quo*.

Many kinds of bond go to make a community.[6] Many different factors may stimulate the first co-operation. Anthropologists see the origin of primitive communities often in terms of co-operation for defence : either self-defence against other communities or the naturally hostile environment; or co-operative defence of some useful territorial position, such as a spring, good hunting grounds, convenient caves or a supply of some useful mineral. Communities of a more sophisticated kind may have similar unifying bonds : a fishing village organised round one occupation, the inhabitants of a united geographical area such as a Greek valley, the possession of some degree of monopoly over

[6] Excellent discussions of the complex issues involved are to be found in Robert Nisbet's, *Twilight of Authority*; de Jouvenel's *Sovereignty*; Peter Laslett's Essay, *The Face to Face Society*; in *Philosophy, Politics and Society, Series One*; in Karl Deutsch's books; and in Raymond Plant's *Community and Ideology*, which is a useful guide to the literature. Details of these books will be found in the Bibliography.

a tradable item such as oil or a canal; all these are likely to contribute to the growth of a local community. Similar economic or intellectual interests may produce a non-geographic community for their protection or advancement, such as guild, Trade Union, or a college. So also shared religious or intellectual faith of a kind which sees merit in community (or is forced to see its need as a result of persecution) may produce Calvinistic communities, Trappist monasteries, or communist cells. Shared functions within an institution which is not itself a community may produce a community, like the 'village' which senior civil servants have created at Whitehall. It is even possible for mere juxtaposition to produce community, though the experience of modern cities shows that often some additional catalyst is needed, beyond simple proximity, to get co-operation started. The catalyst may be an external threat, like foreign bombers or native re-developers, resistance to which compels the recognition of common interests, or sometimes more pacifically-generated common loyalties.'

3. *The Face to Face Society.*

At the heart of many communities is what Laslett[7] calls a 'face-to-face society'; a group whose members share enough experience and enough similarity of feeling for each one to be able with little thought to predict what will happen in various situations, without reference to rules or history books or arbitration panels. The purest example of such a face-to-face community is a closely-knit family. (Those politicians who believe they can rely on shared instincts are treating the nation like a family. Unfortunately for them, the nation is a very different sort of creature.) As two-way communications improve, the actual territorial unity of a face-to-face community becomes a little less important, though not yet wholly unimportant: a family scattered soon loses unity, however much writing or telephoning there may be; and few big companies find it possible successfully to create for long the face-to-face community of a board of directors by means of even the most sophisticated closed-circuit television system.

There is no single defining characteristic of a functioning com-

[7] Op. cit.

munity, other than that its members feel they belong to a community and are accepted as members by those they feel to be their fellows. Race can often be one binding factor; shared experience (though with the important proviso that the experience is similarly interpreted)[8] shared literary or artistic culture; or shared enemies. It is impossible to lay down a single ordering of importance, and results may surprise the unwary. For instance it is probable that the shared hatred of Vietnamese by Cambodians (and *vice versa*) enshrined in history and tradition, will do more to divorce those two newly communist peoples than will shared political outlook to unite them. Men are usually members of several communities at the same time, and sometimes suffer painful conflicts as a result : family loyalties tested by the company ethos; Trades Union obedience *versus* the interests of a local community—such would be familiar examples.

Though it is necessary that the origins of any community lie in a face-to-face society, a community thus originating may spread itself quite widely before people lose the sense of belonging : but there is clearly a trade-off between extension and the intensity of communal feeling. The behaviour of different Trades Unions may illustrate this : in a conflict between national policy and local feeling, it is usual for the sense of national belonging to be vulnerable to the strength of local face-to-face groups in big plants, mines or shipyards. On the other hand, unions which consist of scattered individuals joined only by voluntary adherence to the national rule book may find that they have failed to create much sense of allegience and instead find their members placing loyalty to the union lower in their scale of priorities than loyalty to other, for example local, communities.

4. *Landmarks.*

Of obvious importance to any community are those fixed landmarks to which the sense of belonging attaches itself. The landmarks may be abstract or physical. They may be shared beliefs : in a family that the members are ruled by a blood tie, and that such a tie is important; they may derive from the per-

[8] Lord Windlesham describes how shared experiences *differently* interpreted divide people from each other in Northern Ireland. Lord Windlesham, *Politics in Practice,* (London, 1975) p. 82.

manence of the people concerned: as again, the permanence of
the relationship (compared to most relationships) between the
child and its mother allows love to grow between them. In
local communities, the landmarks may literally be the defining
characteristics of the locality: this may be because these characteristics are involved in some economic unifying factor. (Thus if
you build a barrage and remove the sea from a fishing village,
the community dies unless it moves, or finds some other unifying
trade.) Or, the landmarks may be just the reference points by
which membership is explicitly or implicitly defined. These may
be anything from the sound of bells (which were said once to
define a cockney) to proximity to a football ground, to proximity
to a church, to the existence of a building in which the community
actually lives together. None of these is likely to have been the
original cause of the growth of the community; any of them may
become important tests for the identification of someone as a
community member, and his acceptance by fellow members.
You will have a hard time trying to argue that a man is not a
real Fulham man if he watches the team every Saturday, knows
all the pubs, and knows who Tommy Trinder is, even if the man
in question is black or Irish. Equally, if the team goes bust, the
pubs are replaced with automatic vending machines, and Mr
Trinder goes to live in California, the community will need to
look for other comparable landmarks, and may not find them;
if it does not, people may fall back on cruder labels such as race
or national origin.

5. *Continuity.*

Finally, a community may be bound together by the very way
in which the members express their value of it. This expression
of value is most likely to take the form of a wish that the community should continue, even after deaths of individual members.
Thus all sorts of institutions and mechanisms which try to look
to the future of a community, by caring for important land
marks, saving to make provision for future difficulties, or finding
new ways of handing on the interests and achievements of one
generation to the next, thus acknowledging and renewing a continuing culture, are signs of a healthy community.

Community and the Future

So far, we have argued that any satisfactory account of the human condition must recognise man's need for his fellows, and that without the preservation of healthy communities, the individual loses his humanity. In Part II, we showed that inherent in the Conservative tradition is an understanding that the statesman must preserve the patterns of life which weave themselves into such communities. These patterns and communities are liable to destruction, on the one hand, from those who believe that if anything goes, satisfactory patterns automatically emerge; and, on the other, those who wish to establish their preferred patterns by political force, destroying what exists and imposing a fatal and unnaturally static inflexibility on society. We argued that, seen in this light, the traditional Conservative objectives— the preservation of authority, the belief in tradition, the trust in an underlying and to all intents and purposes unchanging morality, the hostility to dogma and the fear of change—represent the only approach to politics which not only allows the necessary primacy to community, but also provides an effective set of weapons with which to defend it from its enemies. We can therefore now present our first conclusion, that man needs community and that Conservatives are more likely to give it to him than anyone else. But at the beginning of Part I, we promised to do a little more than that. We promised also to argue that the likely course of the future would make Conservatism more relevant and more important rather than less. We painted a rather bleak picture of a world of shortages and tensions, of economic and industrial problems, and of the failure of orthodoxies which still dominate the political scene even if increasing doubts are raised about them. Why do we think that Conservatism not only should, but could, offer the citizen a safe political haven in such a world? Let us draw together some of the different arguments we have deployed and make the case for the future value of Conservative Community. Then we can go on to examine some of the recent political developments which have been most destructive of it, and give examples of approaches to policy compatible with it.

Our dangerous future will find three things in Conservatism which it will need.

First, a world in which, at the very least, economic growth cannot be guaranteed, and in which political philosophies should not be based any more on the assumption that it can, will find in Conservatism an understanding of, and delight in, the increased valuation which must be placed upon stability in order to replace allegiance to growth. Conservatives are not frightened of a society which is only slowly changing; indeed, we believe it to be far preferable to flux, because flux is destructive of community, as we shall argue in the next chapter. We have in our philosophy concepts which will allow the post-growth world to reorganise itself away from philosophies predicted on change, increase and expansion. Tradition is one; unchanging morality is another; respect for order and hierarchy is another. What is more, we think that a return to the fulfilment man can find in a stable community, continuing pretty predictably into the future out of a well-loved past, is anyway much preferable to the fulfillment alleged to result from playing the desperate game of snakes-and-ladders he has to play in the growth-man's world of constantly changing expectations. And Conservatives can offer fulfilment without clamping the citizen onto the iron rack of totalitarian ideology which, though it may be able to exist without economic growth, cannot co-exist with rationality, flexibility, or change of any sort, and which, valuing the individual not at all, makes a mistake as absurd and as dangerous as do the most extreme individual Liberals in the opposite sense.

So, the first future strength of Conservatism is that it is the only approach to politics which is humanly tolerable, but which can also flourish in a stable, post-growth, economic world.[1]

[1] Some of the most perceptive economists, contemplating what will happen when growth can no longer be relied on, produce advice which looks uncannily like the traditional Conservative prescription, though they do not necessarily start from that point. The best recent example is *The Economic Growth Debate—an assessment*—E. J. Mishan, (George Allen and Unwin, 1977).

The second is that, in the dangerous period ahead there is going to be a need for authority, strength and decision. Doing nothing, in the face, say, of rapid industrial decline or violent racial tensions, will be wicked. Conservatism restores the concept of authority to its necessary place in the centre of the political stage without falling into mystical nonsense about it. This will not be the least of the gifts we have to offer. Without us, no one offers a self-confident theory of authority other than the Communists.

Finally, we have in Part I noticed some issues, such as the proliferation of nuclear weapons and the consequently necessary control of civil nuclear programmes, where national control will have to be surrendered to non-national regulatory agencies, with power, if the world is to remain safe. World government, in the sense of centralised world administration, is a nightmare only tolerable to contemplate because it happily seems to get no nearer. But a worldwide agency or police, empowered by authority delegated from nations to use what force is necessary to do the job of regulating stocks of, say, plutonium, and guarding them against either terrorism or the risk of a nuclear nation falling, however temporarily, into the hands of a lunatic, may well not be so far off if we are to live safely. At a more pedestrian level, as we shall argue in the next chapter, in all sorts of different ways the nineteenth-century nation is likely to find its functions of declining importance in a world of regional economies, world-wide trade and communications, and problems shared across borders.

Conservatism is the only philosophy which recognises the danger that the decline of nations brings with it : there will be complex and disturbing effects on the sense of belonging and of co-operation which is necessary to fulfilled life. But Conservatism, while recognising these real dangers, does not regard them as insurmountable because it offers an alternative, or as we could argue, a more natural, object of allegiance : not the politically delineated state, but the naturally grown community —village, district, college, factory, town or fraternity. That is where the mystery lies; it is at this level that the complex process of natural development over time generates those feelings of loyalty, affection, and allegiance better described by a poet than a sociologist, and mysteriously more productive than the energy of a mere collection of individuals. No one can fully explain the magic which enables the fusion of a collection of individuals to release the energies of a community. Often allegiance to shared myths, about leaders, or history, or the future is part of it. What the Conservative sees is that those who thought that such allegiance must only and always attach to the nation, let alone to the organs of the State, were making the mistake of equating nation and community. The two are far different creatures. We respect what Ulysses says in *Troilus and Cressida*:

> 'There is a mystery—with whom relation
> Durst never meddle—in the soul of state,
> Which hath an operation more divine
> Than breath or pen can give expression to.'[2]

But we offer the post-nation-state world a philosophy in which the mystery and the allegiance have a place of honour still, because we believe that they are the words the poet uses to refer to the essential and unplannable complexity of naturally grown communities; but though we recognise why nation and community became confused (we will discuss this further in the next chapter) we recognise that community, and not nation, is primary. We recognise that patriotism is essential—but that patriotism may attach itself to other objects than the nation state.

[2] Shakespeare, *Troilus and Cressida*, Act 3. Scene 3.

CHAPTER FOUR

Community and Nation

1. The Progress towards national community.

What is the relationship between the political nation and the community? If a nation is a community, as perhaps Greek City states may have been or isolated tribes and very small territorially distinct countries, such as, say, Barbados, may still be, then politics, that is the discussion and control of the activities of the national State, disappear, subsumed into the organisation of the community.

Obviously, if the community and the nation are co-extensive, many unpleasant political problems disappear. Shared traditions and culture are likely to be developed to the point where instinct will produce consensus. Shared allegiance to landmarks of various kinds makes their destruction unlikely; attachment to history make its continuance likely. There will, of course, still be problems (particularly about leadership), as there are within families, and they can be very acute indeed: but they are problems which arise within a framework which, used with a minimum of goodwill, provides hope of their solution.

For many years, it looked as if Britain was quite well on the way to aligning the myriad separate communities of the pre-industrial world into one great national community. This would have been a remarkable achievement, and though the unifying processes of the nineteenth and early twentieth century produced the same sort of effects in other nations, Britain by 1914 was probably the furthest advanced in the process, which gave her that extraordinary strength which was expended in the Flanders mud. A magnificent Scott Fitzgerald purple passage on the titanic battle between three of the nations which had been furthest advanced towards national community describes with genius the bonds which unite societies:

'See that little stream—we could walk to it in two minutes. It took the British a month to walk to it—a whole Empire walking very slowly, dying in front and pushing forward behind. And another Empire walked very slowly backward a few inches a day, leaving the dead like a million bloody rugs. No European will ever do that again in this generation . . .

This took religion and years of plenty and tremendous sureties and the exact relation that existed between the classes. The Russians and Italians weren't any good on this front. You have to have a whole-souled sentimental equipment going back further than you could remember. You had to remember Christmas, and postcards of the Crown Prince and his fiancée, and little cafés in Valence, and beer gardens in Unter den Linden and weddings at the *mairie* and going to the Derby, and your grandfather's whiskers.'

'General Grant invented this kind of battle at Petersburg in sixty-five.'

'No he didn't—he just invented mass butchery. This kind of battle was invented by Lewis Carroll, and Jules Verne and whoever wrote *Undine*, and country deacons bowling and *marraines* in Marseilles and girls seduced in the back lanes of Würtenberg and Westphalia . . .'[1]

The development of a national community in Britain had many elements. A language shared between most (though in the nineteenth century far from all) of the inhabitants of the nation was one element; shared experience of Empire, usually attached to symbolic incidents (the capture of Quebec, the Indian Mutiny, the relief of Mafeking); shared success in economic terms; steady religious, political and cultural landmarks (the Monarchy, the Church, Parliament—even though the suffrage did slowly alter—the law and legal institutions, Milton and Shakespeare). The destruction of village communities by the industrial revolution led many, slum dwellers in meaningless new urban sprawls, to look to the nation instead to provide symbols for their allegiance and catalysts for the sense of belonging. The development of economic and phychological theory based on the individual, not the community, as the

---

[1] F. Scott Fitzgerald, *Tender is the Night*, (The Grey Walls Press, London, 1953) p. 135-6. Tim Raison, M.P., uses this quotation in a rather similar way in his *Why Conservative?* (Penguin, London 1964).

primary unit both caused and reflected the fact of those thousands of labourers walking from their villages to work in the new
artificial towns.

In spite of all this, however, the nation did not ever get very
close to being a community. Pre-1914 newspapers or Barbara
Tuchman's '*The Proud Tower*'[2] show how far the Edwardian
world really was from a golden age, and how far Britain was,
even then, from having achieved a national community. And
now the process of integration seems to have gone into reverse.
We look at the two most dramatic reversals in the next section.

2. *Scotland and Ulster*

Today, the whole question of the proper boundaries of the
nation has been revived by Scottish nationalism, to a lesser
extent Welsh nationalism, and conflict in Ulster. Even if we
were to seek to continue the process of eighteenth- and nineteenth-
century nation-building to the point where the political boundaries came nearer to co-incidence with the real boundaries of
our natural community, we now are faced with the seventeenth-
century question : What are those boundaries? What is the
nation?

During the period of Empire, the success offered by the State
apparatus of the United Kingdom was so great, and the world
so much defined in terms of competition with culturally similar
Europeans for control over wholly alien peoples, that obvious
groupings of peoples tended to come together. The first impact
of modern communications and nationally based education had
the same effect. Today, the United Kingdom State has not
seemed to offer so much to its people, and their allegiance to it,
offered any shadow of an alternative, has declined.[3] Again, we
are not competing around the world against Belgians, French,
Italians, Dutch, Portuguese and Spanish in quite the same way
as we were in the Imperial steeplechase : commercial rivalry is
world wide, rather less with other Europeans than with relative
newcomers such as the Japanese and Americans. This, along

[2] London, 1966.
[3] The evidence of falling participation in General Elections since 1950 is just
as likely to be evidence of declining support for or interest in the West-
minster-based State as it is to be a specific protest against the electoral
arrangements, as is argued by some electoral reformers.

with the traumas of two European wars, and a world dominated by non-European super-powers, makes tight groupings of Europeans against each other, whether British, German, Slav or Latin, rather pointless. The reasons for the total adherence of Scotland to London rather than Paris or Oslo slip into history; and the further development of modern transport, surface transport having initially bound the island closer, greatly strengthen overseas links.

Thus Englishmen would be very unwise to underestimate, in particular, Scottish nationalism. It reflects some of the changing realities of the world. Certainly, some of its supporters are very similar to the protest voters of the Liberal Party or the National Front; but that is only to say that the latter are embryonic English nationalists seeking (and not finding) effective ways of demonstrating their own doubts about the United Kingdom State governed from Westminster. Certainly, increased economic success within present national boundaries will restore some allegiance. But the underlying trends are those which are likely to weaken the kind of nations created in the last two centuries: the sense of belonging, never solely the attribute of nations, will be likely to return to smaller communities of which Scotland may be one—though a single Scotland from the Orkneys to the Border is merely a newly invented eighteenth century nation itself. Like some Serbia, it is unlikely to be a unit which for long inspires more than antiquarian loyalties.[4]

Thus we should not necessarily fear, as if we were still at war with Philip of Spain, the rise of a hostile power to our north, whose legions will threaten Sunderland or Blackpool whenever we complain about the price of oil. Such a throw-back Scottish nation would not last long; the bonds are not there in Western Europe out of which we may forge new nations. We should recognise that—for England, Scotland, Wales, and all Ireland—conditions have so changed that new relationships between regions are desirable and possible. We must beware, as Conservatives, the systems-expert's attempts to assign loyalties according to what appears to him administratively most rational; our approach should be to attempt to find new natural building-blocks of communities to group together as best we can.

[4] Conor Cruise O'Brien has had the courage to point out that the same would probably be true of a belatedly united Ireland.

There are still likely, for example, to be stronger national bonds for many decades inside the traditional nation, defined as the United Kingdom, than there are within any emerging European unit—particularly as the government of the present community is so inept, and its boundaries anyway constantly expand. There are, between England, Wales and Scotland, many genuine ties to set against the equally genuine separatist feeling. But what would Westminster do if a majority of Scottish MPs were Nationalists, if their demands for separation were confirmed by a referendum? Fight them? Of course not. We would then have, as peoples within the United Kingdom, to settle down together to hammer out a new division of political responsibilities and powers within these islands.

Perhaps Scotland *should* for example have representatives on EEC bodies, and perhaps all Britons would benefit thereby; perhaps when we got down to the figures, Scotland *would* see more to gain from continued financial links with England and Wales— since the industrial links are so close as to be indissoluble. Perhaps on the other hand a federal solution, within one, old-style, nation but with virtually separate governments in various provinces would be the answer. It is very likely that, if not as a result of this particular wave of interest, then of the next or the next, some new settlement will emerge. Devolutionists are right to recognise this—though they are likely to be unsuccessful in their attempts to head off feelings which derive from fundamental emotions, to do with belonging, loyalty and trust or otherwise of traditional rivals, by means of further imposed administrative plans.

All the evidence is that most Scots have no interest in or knowledge of the present extensive devolution from Westminster. Somehow—and who can blame them?—that is not quite what they are talking about. But the devolutionists are wrong, in so far as they regard their objective as being the tactical concession of devolutionist counters in order to protect a sacred national *status quo*. It is the basic communities which are primary, and valued by the Conservative—not the political groupings.

These developments should not terrify Conservatives. The underlying communities, the traditions of living, the old institutions and patterns, are more important than the political boundaries, even though, for Englishmen at least, the political boundaries have been stable for so long that they are inextricably bound up in the way we live. England will not disintegrate—and, if we think seriously about new and looser groupings within our islands, it is quite likely that 2027 will see some form of United Kingdom still extant, though by 2077 (cataclysms apart) one might expect to see the nation states dissolve into some European entity.

The process must ultimately be the only prospect for hope in Ulster. The inherent instability of the two minorities in Ireland—Protestants in a united Ireland, Catholics in a separate Northern Ireland—means that no solution based on either of those two modern political entities can be long stable. Terrorism, torture, heroism, ballads, ancient feuds, triumphs and defeats make immeasurably more difficult any solution, since patterns of life revolve around them, and a culture rather like that of an ancient Homeric or Anglo-Saxon warrior makes them its foundation—a culture infinitely more difficult to assimilate into a stable, co-operative society than communities merely disagreeing about political ends. It is like trying to assimilate Tacitus's Germans into the legal and commercial framework of the Roman Empire. It is probably true now that there is nothing to be offered to the Provisional IRA which they could accept—or nothing they would take which they would count as victory—because theirs is now a culture of warfare, like that of the Apaches or Hitler's SS. It is difficult to see how any modern society can do anything other than get as near as it can to eliminating them— but unless radical thinking continues in the quest for new ways of making the old feuds irrelevant to the majority, there will always be enough new recruits from that majority who, accepting the old feuds, carrying them on in the old way, will ensure that for every terrorist you kill, another is born. Thus it is no good treating with the terrorists themselves, any more than it was with Hitler : their culture is not sufficiently similar to that of people we call civilised to make the concept of agreement with them comprehensible. But without an unremitting search for new political initiatives, it will be equally pointless defeating existing terrorists. Even the process of political initiative and failure is better than static hopelessness : each change helps to undermine the apparent inevitability, to their members, of the old existing, pathological, communities. Change helps to destroy communities. When the communities are sound, change is therefore to be treated warily; when they are unsound, flux is to be welcomed.

CHAPTER FIVE

The Decline of Community

1. *Industrialism.*

Whatever progress may once have been made towards the goal of national community in the United Kingdom has long been in reverse. This presents dangers, doubtless, but not insuperable ones. What should worry a Conservative is not just that the progress of Britain towards becoming a community has been reversed (we were never very near to its achievement) but that the maintenance of *any* community inside the boundaries of the nation has become more difficult; the movement has been towards an atomised society of individuals faced with the growing institutions of the state. Destruction of the old, pre-industrial communities, and the failure of the central bureaucracy of the state, standing increasingly alone amongst the competing individualists of the Liberal society, to make of the nation a satisfactory substitute for them (except under the extreme pressures of war), had long been predicted by Conservative writers who made a golden age, naturally enough, of the only alternative they had known, the medieval world. Writers like Adam Müller, even reactionaries like the Vicomte de Bonald, poets like Coleridge, had been predicting the dangers since early in the nineteenth century. As John Weiss writes in his *Conservatism in Europe*[1] 'Long before the left became concerned with alienation and economics in modern industrial urban society, these conceptions were basic to Conservative thought.'

The modern Conservative, though more likely, in his moments of nostalgia, to seek his golden age in Walter Scott, or in the quiet, non-industrial world of small-town Regency life depicted

[1] Thames and Hudson, (London 177), p. 49.

in Jane Austen than in free trading Manchester, must recognise the gains made in one direction by the destruction of the world of medieval communities. Feudalism and the temporal aspects of the Christianity which supported it were, after all, a form of all embracing political theory sometimes imposed and maintained with violence and cruelty. But the carelessness of the consequences, which Conservatives predicted would flow from the destruction of natural community, destruction which was inherent in the new Liberal order, produced dire results—one of which was the pathologically nostalgic reaction of Fascism. Our task is to rebuild community, in a non-pathological form, before, *faute-de-mieux*, people join what they can and be damned to the consequences.

People must belong somewhere : if the State destroys communities which are benign, and can co-exist with it, then communities will arise which are not benign, and cannot co-exist with it. Such are the extremist political parties of left and right which defile our politics; such, in some moods, are our Trades Unions. The task for the Conservative is to show how community can be restored, without threatening the State; and to equip himself with an understanding of what the State must and must not do to make this possible. Before we come to what the State can do, we must set out what it is still doing which it should not do, if community is to survive. First, it should fear inflation like the social plague it is. Second, it should beware of the casual clearance of landmarks without which communities cannot live.

2. *Inflation.*

It is possible to imagine a world in which a rapid fall in the value of the currency was so perfectly matched by changes in the value of everything else that no social strains would ensue. It would be a complicated Heraclitean world, in which we would have to treat flux in the way we are accustomed now to treat stationariness. It is presumably only possible to envisage this situation for a nation which is self-contained—unless all its trading partners were in similar states of flux. But what I shall be discussing in this chapter is the kind of inflation we know in a Britain needing to trade with other nations which have different rates of inflation (usually less than ours) or no inflation at all.

A prolonged decline in the value of money in a society whose expectations and institutions are predicated on its stability has a number of fundamental effects. First, since the currency is one of the primary State institutions, the failure to maintain its value is a continuing source of disillusionment with the effectiveness of the State as a whole and the government which controls its institutions. Only when the value of money is roughly stable is the individual person able to use it for those calculations of comparative worth which are the basis of his economic transactions with his fellows; once instability is introduced, and price-rises do not reflect any information (such as increased scarcity, increased quality—even irritating information such as the existence of a monopolist), then he is bound to be forced back to direct rule-of-thumb comparisons between one good and another —to the beginnings of a return to a barter economy. For instance, people may start talking not about the price of housing, but about the share of their earnings which they spend on housing compared to other goods; which is a process of valuation in terms of the other goods on which they spend. Even if wages are indexed to inflation in some way, they are likely to be indexed in relation to some average 'shopping basket' of goods which people are alleged by some arm of government to buy;[2] however skilfully this is done, it means that someone else is making a judgement, most likely based on generalisations of past behaviour, about what the wage earner wants to buy before he does so. No one, after all, is the average shopper.

But it is not necessary to be so complicated. The State undertakes, in writing, on every banknote, to maintain a stable currency, and it fails to do so. The result is the importation of injustice into every debtor-creditor relationship where repayment is made of an original sum; the penalisation of those who save for the future; the growth of non-productive money-making by those who are skilful enough to manipulate the trust of those who believe the Government when it says it will maintain a stable currency; the destruction of institutions and communities that rely on accumulated savings, such as universities or charities, which have to become part of the State bureaucracy to survive,

[2] This is how the British Retail Prices Index is constructed.

and, as our present arrangements are ordered, the constant, dubiously legal, increase in taxes.[3] More difficult to quantify is the disappearance of a thousand tiny but significant landmarks and their replacement by constantly changing figures: no one can be sure nowadays what a stamp costs, or a fine for pulling the communication cord on the railway; it would be impossible now for an institution to become known by its cost like the penny post. No one knows what to expect. The accompaniment of all this by the destruction of an unusually old coinage in Britain—so that the incidental and considerable value of the existence of a national landmark[4] which had survived for a century and a half was lost at the same time—means that the currency has lost what was once one of its primary roles as an ever-present unifier of the nation and token of governmental good faith.

Is this government's fault? Or is it a natural disaster like a plague which can fall on any nation and undermine State and community with no one to blame? No one would argue that, at the cost of the loss of other objectives, government could not have kept the currency stable. A balance has to be struck. An institution does not have to work perfectly to work well enough. Which objectives of government would have suffered from the attempt to make the institution of the currency work better? In a world where productivity increases, stability means increasing the supply of money roughly in line with productivity. Why does government do more? Overwhelmingly of course, for two reasons. First, in pursuit of the recurrent delusion that it has made the breakthrough and discovered how to produce growth (or do away with unemployment), it may be engaged in one of the periodic dramatic experiments with overall 'demand'—that is, an experiment with people's expectations and trust. 'Demand' is an aggregate of the hopes of a huge number of people. Such hopes are altered by giving or taking away currency which these people are foolish enough to believe has value in goods. Every

[3] If inflation speeds up a bit more, the Government will start to lose from this process, since the money demanded will slip more in value before it is paid than indexed wages will have increased. W. Guttman and P. Meehan: *The Great Inflation, Germany 1919-1923,* (Farnborough, Hants, 1975), describes how this happened during the German inflation.

[4] The Romans systematically used their coinage to court the loyalty of subjects of the Empire. See Michael Grant, *Roman History from Coins,* (Cambridge 1958), p. 13.

operation of this kind disorientates people a little more—or raises their distrust of the currency and so of government. This experiment is likely to involve a large increase in the money supply and to be followed, when the elastic pulls us back to the underlying growth rate, by the necessity of taking some of the excess money away from people again. Every time, however, that the process occurs, expectations are further aroused, and distrust further engendered. Like a doctor who finds that by the time his patient has begun to respond, the treatment is so overwhelming as to be more dangerous than the disease, so do governments regularly find that by the time they see a response of any kind from the economy, the increase in available money is far greater than the value of the goods the country can produce to match it. To get any significant response at all in the late 1970s, policy changes have to be so violent as to make the whole approach too dangerous for a responsible government to contemplate its use.

Secondly, the Government may have been pushed by some powerful lobby into an attempt to engage in various activities which need resources—such as men, or the goods men produce, or factories—of which the supply is limited, without first taking them away from some other employment. It will characteristically do this by running up a deficit of expenditure over income from taxes and loans, and guaranteeing to supply the money needed. The activities concerned need not be directly under its control; fighting a war is likely to be inflationary, but so is guaranteeing money to people in various trades, coal-mining, ship-building or motor manufacture, for example, which have not managed to persuade people to provide them with money voluntarily (by freely buying their goods). In the latter case, the activity is inflationary, unless the money has been taken away from someone else first (which would normally have an equal and opposite effect on employment elsewhere).

Third, there are times when, for reasons quite outside its control, the standard of living has to fall in a nation because of the activities of those with whom it trades—who demand higher prices for their goods, or sell no goods at all. Wars which involve blockades are extreme examples of this; the oil embargo was a recent case. If the government did nothing in such a case, prices of other goods (and wages of those who produce them) would have to fall, or people would not be able to sell their output and so would lose employment. If firms and Trades Unions prevent real wages falling for those in work, then higher unemployment is inevitable for the rest. In a situation like this there is no way of avoiding a decline in the average standard of living, though there may be ways of preventing all the strain being taken by those who go wholly out of work (which is how Britain is doing it) if we are willing to attack the institutions which try to keep wages always rising in relation to prices.

So the hoped-for gains which government trades off against loss of stability of the currency are those promised, first, by growth theory—which is likely to be imaginary anyway—and, second, other objectives, such as subsidising sections of industry, which may from time to time become government policy via the political process, but which Ministers are unwilling to pay for by confiscation of the necessary funds through the tax system. As to the first trade-off, it is illusory: nothing is gained. The second is more problematic. Why should governments not cause inflation—with the risks to stability described above—in pursuit, say, of more spending on better hospitals? In pursuit of such a goal, what does it matter if inflation inconveniences a large number of people? It might be worth getting the hospitals at the cost of difficulties elsewhere.[5]

In fact, the choice is illusory. Inflation threatens stability so completely that the State will find all sorts of unexpected and chaotic developments preventing it from building its hospitals, such as strife in the building industry as employers take the brunt of expectations raised and disappointed by the inflation. No one who has worked in industry in the last few years can believe that a period of rapid inflation could possibly form the basis for the breakthrough to growth; and few who have worked in Whitehall do not see how damaging inflation is to that authority without which no government programme can be completed successfully. Energies are all turned inward, as group protects itself against group; customers and tax-payers despair as prices and taxes soar unpredictably; morale falls all round.

---

[5] This argument was fashionable for a time in socialist circles before 1974, since it was believed that the relatively well-off, and the bourgeoisie with its savings, suffered more from inflation than the workers. The said workers, however, know better.

The hospitals, if started, are abandoned half finished, like public monuments in Sukarno's Indonesia. The theory does not work.

Inflation, then, has had far reaching effects as a solvent of stability; to use the CIA word, it is a most efficient de-stabiliser.

3. *Legislative Flux*

But inflation is not alone; if it were, there might be more antibodies to it in the body politic. Other infections have also been weakening community resistance. First and foremost has been the legislative aspect of ever-expanding government—a remedy for which we have already argued the need. Just as ministerial reputations are often based upon the increases they secure in the spending of their Departments, so they can also be based on the passage of major statutes. Just as the virility of a spending Department is shown in how well it does in the annual bargaining with the Treasury; so it is also demonstrated in the official and ministerial legislative committees which apportion legislative time. And just as the House of Commons has long since ceased effectively to check the growth of spending (if it ever was really interested in such an objective) so it has only weakly resisted playing its part in the legislative landslide—and then only because back-bench members would like more time for their own Solonian experiments (and for their holidays).

Such is the instability of a modern British Government, with General Elections coming on average once every three years since the Second World War, that a certain amount of this legislative productivity does not much effect the citizen directly : the new law is overturned before it is established. However even then, as, for example, in the famous pensions case, where five Bills preceded Mrs Castle's of 1974 and five more will doubtless succeed it, someone feels the strain : in this case the companies, accountants, and civil servants who spend decades in virtually un-productive but very difficult work preparing for each new Bill as if it was the last.

Other cases have more pervasive effects. The most obvious category, and the most directly damaging, is the annual or twice-yearly finance acts which can alter at a stroke of the pen the whole framework of life : a sudden fashion for steeply pro-gressive tax rates may upset a lifetime's plans; a change in taxation of savings or in the right to bequeath or to give; a new allowance against tax or its abolition—all these can mean that behaviour which has up to then been legal, and indeed prudent and wise, becomes illegal. In a society where costs and benefits valued in money take the place of governmental fiat for most of the daily transactions of life, the effect of constant changes in the financial rules has much the same disorienting effect as the rapid replacement of one fiat by another in an arbitrary dictatorship. It is one of the boasts of a free society that it avoids just this kind of disorientation—but, in the effect of what they do on society, fashionable economists are much more like the less satisfactory Julio-Claudian Emperors than they might care to notice. The effect on individual people is Pavlovian, and results finally in failure to respond to any stimuli except the most extreme; for companies and other organised bodies (voluntary association or charities, for example) similar alterations may result in well-laid plans becoming valueless overnight, or even in the whole purpose of the association disappearing. Another $2\frac{1}{2}\%$ on this or that product's VAT sounds like an operation of a technical kind to the civil servants whose interest is to calculate the revenue which will accrue or the 'demand' that will be diminished; he does not, and cannot, estimate the social costs of the change in terms of wasted expectations and industrial disruption. No pressure group, however strong, can count on their ability to prevent arbitrary changes of this kind—partly because the secrecy of the budget process, and the speed with which the Finance Acts are subsequently passed into law, are both designed to allow the Prime Minister and the Chancellor the greatest possible freedom to act without constraints. The history of regional development grants and allowances, their alteration and the movement towards Ministerial discretion in their application, shows the powerlessness of both the TUC and CBI to persuade governments of the obvious benefit of stability —any stability—in an area dear to both organisations' hearts.

The same process is at work in every area, and the psychological effect is cumulative. What is more, there is no guarantee that the passing of a law whose implementation needs resources of men or money will be followed by the provision of such resources. Established patterns may be overturned in favour of new ones; but the new pattern may never become established

E

because the wandering searchlight of governmental interest has by then moved elsewhere, leaving the affected area with little more than a new law and a sense of confusion. The Children and Young Persons Act, 1969, was one of these : a fine argument can be made for the intentions of the Act if it had been implemented in the ways which cost money; but the money was not there. Such an Act, which affects permanently the chances of a reasonable life for some tens of thousands of our citizens, should be a major event, behind which the whole Government ranges its influence, and whose implications for expenditure are spelt out in the Act. It should not be just the result of the fact that the Home Office with a civilised Minister comes to the top of the legislative queue, that a pressure group has proposals ready, and that the single effective legislative House, after brief debate, has affixed its seal.

Industrial relations, housing, industry policy, welfare, education systems—the list covers all the main areas of life. Indeed in the payment of cash benefits the system relies upon the fact that the flux has produced such confusion in the minds of potential recipients that a good proportion of them will never catch up : for, if all benefits were fully taken up, it would be impossible for them to be paid without overturning completely the estimates of expected public expenditure.

The cost of all these changes is never quantified. How *does* one quantify a sense of regret and disorientation on the part of millions of people at say, local government boundary changes? One cannot; whereas one can (or thinks one can) quantify the savings in manpower derived from the rationalisation of organisations which is supposed (supposed) to ensue. The former is a public good, the latter a private good of some department or other pressure group; the former has no defence, the victory for modernisation of the latter is part of the process of government.

So it is that the stability, the landmarks, on which community life relies, fall victim to a process of government become ever more arbitrary. Rather like a primitive tribesman surrounded by a physical world which he sees in terms of mysterious and unpredictable demigods and imps, whom he can only, blindly, propitiate, so the citizens and the community today cannot be sure that anything is safe from Leviathan, if Leviathan, turns his attention that way. So you own a house? A motorway may go through it. You have saved your money? We will make it worthless by inflation. You work for private enterprise? Just wait. You want your children to go to the school you went to? It will not exist by then. So do the landmarks go down, and settled life gives way to *anomie.*

4. *The Destruction of Landmarks,*

The destruction of familiar buildings is only one form of the process, but it is a particularly disorienting one,[6] particularly if done on a piecemeal basis which never seems to end. A town so destroyed creates a sense of disappointment, of personal loss which weakens that community in ways undreamt of in the discussions when the local council or the Minister decided to allow development. The costs must be looked for in quite un-expected ways—in ways related to the weakening of the community and the disorientation of individuals. Primarily, of course, they must be looked for in a weakening of the acceptance of the community by its new members: how *can* they accept it when their expectations of what it will continue to be are continually betrayed? We must look for the origins of juvenile crime not only in terms of the stability of the home, but also in terms of what the community offers in the way of being 'home' itself. Who cares about smashing windows in a block of which nobody is fond, of which nobody ever will be fond? It is nothing to do, or little to do, with designing more beautiful or functional blocks —people, given time, can adapt the most unpromising material into the framework for a real community. The solution lies in counting the cost of disorientation itself. Since this cannot yet be done directly, the next best thing is to make arbitrary change more difficult. We have discussed how this might be done at Westminster; complete proposals for slowing down legislation should encompass local government too.

All sorts of other landmarks are relevant. A devilish Fu Manchu, engaged on a plan to leave Britain feeling angry, bewildered, and fragmented, could do worse than to start by

[6] It is particularly damaging, of course, if new developments are designed to embody the precepts of grand theorists of architecture who actually *welcome* the destruction of tradition and of natural community. See pages 142 ff, below, for further discussion of this.

abolishing familiar weights and measures, currency, policemen's uniforms, postage stamp designs, letter box colours, radio and television programmes, brand names, modes of address, and so on—before he undertook the serious work of disruption by turning the welfare system upside down and the Trades Union law inside out. He would rely on the fact that good arguments could be made for each change taken separately, and that the pressure groups in favour of change would feel more passionately that they had the truth than would their opponents.

This may sound like an argument for preserving society like the fly in Herrick's amber. It is not. It is an argument that there ought to be a severe limitation on the speed of change with regard to those laws, regulations, and customs which directly affect how people live—if we value the stability of communities. At the moment there is no such limitation, and, on the contrary, those obstacles to change—such as Parliamentary procedure or the inviolability of personal property or rights (such as a house or job)—are being steadily eroded. In this process many of the old Liberal defences against arbitrary government—usually described as personal rights—have been surrendered (for instance in the steady advance in the use of compulsory purchase or of governmental alterations in 'demand' for men's work).

Conservatives believe that to attempt to set up such rights again, and to hope that the State, over-mighty as it is, will regard them, is by itself utopian. Those rights, and other limitations, must find their protectors in revivified communities which will maintain the limitation of the State which Conservatives wish to effect. It is no good just cutting heads off the hydra if they are to grow again as fast. We must seek arrangements which will stop the State's expansion again in the future. That can only be by filling the vacuum between State and alienated individual with communities in which the individual participates, against which he appeals to the State, and amongst whom the State arbitrates, but which do not look to the State for their origin or substance. The necessary level of allegiance to the State to enable it to do its job of arbitration will follow, if it exercises its proper role efficiently—but only if the concept of allegiance *itself* is protected and encouraged at the level where its occurrence is natural : in the community.

CHAPTER SIX

Community and Corporate State

1. The Conservative Community

All approaches to politics have their pathology. Indeed, over-arching theory of any kind has an inherent tendency towards its own particular pathological state—as Party, Vanguard, chosen race, defender of the classical formulation, or whoever is in charge, tries with increasing desperation to cut down reality to the size of their favoured Procrustean bed of theory. That is why Conservatives fear over-arching theory even when the latter looks beneficent. Let us suppose some genius *did* invent a plan of society which suited human nature perfectly, founded on a political philosophy which explained[1] everything exactly. Let us suppose this wonderful plan to be adopted. What would happen? The plan itself would soon affect people and change their ideas, so that they were not the same as those for whom the plan was designed; the philosophy would soon be criticised from directions which could not have been predicted before its triumph. It is not a matter of conducting the search for a perfect theory more efficiently: no theory of social organisation *can* ever be perfect. The last piece can never be fitted into the puzzle without force.

So we seek an approach to social organisation which has the greatest possible protection against the pathology of the forcible imposition of theory on people. Seeking this, we propose that since no theory of organisation is complete, trust in this kind of theory should be abandoned. All that can be done is to preserve conditions in which we can see that people are able to develop natural patterns of living. These are most likely to be found in

---

[1] The notion is impossible, not only because of human intellectual limitations, but also because it is a misunderstanding of scientific explanations—a misunderstanding of which Marx is guilty—to think that they *can* be complete, like jig-saw puzzles. They are more like good moves in a game of chance: the best we can do, knowing what we know in a world where we can never know everything.

the moderate sized communities which always emerge if allowed the chance. Such communities will be of many and varied sorts, both at work and for living. The State must regulate the inter-action of communities, and must act in defence of basic moral principles when these are threatened within a community. Liberal theory is defective because it leaves nothing between individual and State, and fails to see that no underlying natural morality, without which free competition will be intolerable, can survive long in the (anyway imaginary) world of individualists which they claim to admire. Nonetheless, much of the early Liberal political thought is still useful to the Conservative. This is because the present battle to be fought by Conservatives is for limitation of the role of the State, so that individuals may live naturally again; early Liberals were engaged in a similar battle, though they wrongly proposed the life of the solitary individual as the state of nature, and thought that without the State it could be restored.

Thus it is that the Conservative supports private property, as the best source of independent strength against the over-expansion of the state, and the surest source of stability in a community.

So also he values a clear and relatively unchanging framework of statute law, as guarantor of stability against destabilising legis-lative flux. So, again, he fears inflation like death.

So also, there are many things whose value he recognises which have no place in Liberal theory: continuity of institutions and the physical environment; tradition; the sense of history and belonging—all of which, necessarily restricting the individual in the interest of the community, are objects of the Liberal's hostility.

But one item, fundamental to Liberal thinking, needs to be injected into any Conservative society, because it is the serum which wards off our particular pathology. The serum is direct access by the citizen to, and control over, the machinery of the State—in the words of the United Nations Charter (did ever a Charter describe so well the exact opposite of the majority of its members' behaviour?): 'every one has the right to take part in the government of his country, directly or through freely chosen representatives.' Our pathology, against which this serum gives protection, is the corporate state. Let us look briefly at what is meant by this phrase—now fast becoming meaningless as it is used by all and sundry to describe anything they do not like about the government—and what relation corporatism has with the Conservative tradition.

2. *Corporatism.*

A corporate state is one where you cannot make a distinction which makes sense between the apparatus of the State and the organisation of communities within the boundaries of the nation. In a corporate state life is lived in a society where every group is a building block of a single edifice; where membership of one group, say a family, implies a set relationship with another group, say a village or commune, which implies another relationship with some larger fiefdom. All the bonds in this molecular structure are of equal strength, and none can be altered without a challenge to the whole. Normally, such corporate life is arranged in clear hierarchical form, like feudalism, with strictly defined rights and duties constituting the bonds between each level.

At a simple and primitive stage of human development, such a society, providing at least stability and some measure of efficiency amongst surrounding barbarism, may be all that can be achieved. As soon, however, as sufficient surplus wealth, concentrated power and central organisation has developed, for whatever reason, at the top of the pyramid, so that the king becomes more than merely the grandest cog in the machine, the tendency develops for him to claim the unfettered powers of the modern State. Then the structure must be destroyed or become very dangerous. The danger stems from the fact that if the condition of those lower down the hierarchy alters from one in which their duties to their immediate superiors are balanced by rights that can be claimed against those same superiors, to a condition in which, in addition, they are subject to the new free ranging power of the State against which they have no means of claiming reciprocal rights, those lower beings become virtual slaves to that new State power; moreover, those one away from the top are transformed from being the last tier amongst tiers of equal importance in a pyramidical structure, to the single group with access to the new, rogue power of the king. They are transformed from barons to courtiers.

When the State has emerged, and the organisation of society

is still the simple corporatist hierarchy, the result is the corporate state, where the citizen is represented only by the head of whatever community he works or lives in—and that representation only carries as far as the layer above—while all are subject to the downward, uncheckable, power of the State. Normally, the State takes advantage of some mystical theory, such as divine right, or some sub-Hegelian sophistry such as the State's supposed representation of the collective spirit, to justify this. The dangers to the citizen, and the attractions to the King, of a society where the people still live in feudal subjection, but where the King no longer acknowledges his feudal responsibilities, is one of the themes of those historical plays in which Shakespeare marvellously dissects the different ideas of kingship. Machiavelli's brilliant little essay 'The Prince' showed such newly freed kings what could be done : many were delighted to do it.

Even if worked with goodwill, such a system would be impossible to keep on the rails, manned by the sons of Adam : every group becomes an arena for some little Hitler; no procedure exists for replacing the lunatic or corrupt. Control of the State becomes the object of every power-hungry psychiatric case; the result is, too often, simply barbaric tyranny. Nazi corporatism was of this kind; Marxist states frequently degenerate into it since the justification it provides for the unchecked privileges of the Communist Party as it guides us to Utopia is an attractive way of providing, for the servants of the state, powers over the rest of society not balanced by reciprocal duties.

And in practical terms, the Marxists like corporate organisation for non-Party members : the division of society into small groups reporting to each other is a good way of organising a police state, a fact which appeals greatly to the guides along that particular route to bliss.

It is easy to see how the corporate state is a pathology of Conservatism. Indeed, men of the utmost good-will in the Conservative tradition have veered too near it on occasion.[2] Many of our earliest sages, such as Burke, because they saw the

[2] For an excellent account of the corporatist strand in Conservative thinking see Nigel Harris, *Competition and the Corporate Society, British Conservatives, the State and Industry, 1945-64,* (London 1972). Weiss, op. cit., is also useful, though his greater knowledge of Fascism than Conservatism makes him see the pathology only, and not the rest of the tradition.

undoubted loss of stability and of civilisation which would stem from unfettered liberalism, harked back to the feudal or semi-feudal stability of the past; but the attempt to reimpose the relationships of feudalism once the modern state had emerged would have produced dangers worse than those which Burke and his friends were rightly trying to avoid.

The truth is that it is, as usual, the attempt to convert a single insight into grand theory which says 'there is a single form of community, in which all must be impelled to live and work, and which is the alpha and omega of all political and social organisation' which produces the trouble. In this case, the social insight which is basic to the Conservative tradition, is that tolerable life or work is only possible in a community of human scale in the organisation of which its members should participate if they are to feel that they belong. The grand theory of corporatism is the organised basis for an old enemy—arbitrary tyranny.

What the Conservative argues is this: 'Let us have *no* grand theory—but allow men and women, working, living, and playing, the stability and the raw materials to live properly.' It is a matter of a swing in the balance—away from the atomised individual, away from mass class-solidarity, away from potentially violent self-protective groups—back towards natural community.

The serum which can protect the body politic against the corporate state is, as we have said, access to and control over the State directly, not by his feudal superior, Trades Union boss or CBI delegate but by the citizen himself. To gather such delegates together in a Parliament of Interests, as has sometimes been proposed, would merely formalise the exclusion of the individual from any chance of direct relationship with the State, and would not limit it. The Liberal apparatus, invented to wrest power from kings, remains, in the shape of its descendent, representative democracy, a good machine for keeping the State from absorption by corporate interests, who would then use its power for their own benefit. It needs significant strengthening and revitalising, as we have argued. But let no Conservative fear that there is no other course than towards the Liberal, Marxist, or corporate state. There is, and it is a practical course: the Conservative course.

E*

CHAPTER SEVEN

From Philosophy to Action

A future full of bleak industrial prospects, but not without hope for a prosperity based on skills, on near self-sufficiency in food, and total self-sufficiency in energy; the old social democratic and Keynesian Conservative parties of government declining, bereft of a workable idea of what they should do in power; Liberalism and Marxism both flawed, neither tallying with reality, but both inspiring dedicated sects; separate and contradictory factions all, in aggregate, pushing for a bigger role for the state—but none with a theory of how to control their new Leviathan; a defunct constitution allowing the headless monster thus created to spread havoc amongst the patterns of living necessary for civilised society: against this strange but not necessarily ruinous landscape we put forward the claims of the Conservative tradition to offer one banner at least behind which reasonable people may gather.

The Conservative insight, alone of the major political traditions, is the understanding that, in this world at least, no final theory of how man should live or society be organised is intellectually or morally respectable. This accepted, what matters is to observe how men successfully have lived, and to agree, as the result of such observation, that Aristotle was right: man is a political animal, an animal that lives in a πόλις, a social organisation whose limits and structure are of a scale which he can understand and in which he can participate, or, as we have used the word, a community.

What the Conservative must do first—and it is the easiest part of his difficult task—is so to bind Leviathan that communities may once again find in the world the predictability and the stability they need for growth and survival. Then he must look at the derelict cities and the industrial waste lands, the soulless strip developments and dead new towns, and address himself to the question : what is it here that prevents the natural tendency of men and women, even in difficult conditions, to group themselves together for mutual benefit into some sort of community? The answer, which will never be easy, and will involve many false starts, will be different in different situations. But this approach, which is to assume that the people there, given a chance, will themselves know best how to organise themselves, is fundamental. This book is not an attempt at a detailed manifesto for the Conservative or any other party in the years ahead. It is something different; namely an attempt to show that there is something for the Conservative to aim for, to believe in, something which is a continuation of his traditions, still relevant for the future. He is not just the grudging seceder of new territory mapped out by others, nor the permanent voice of caution and delay in an everlasting dialect between progress and reaction.

He does, indeed, advance what are, to him, unanswerable criticisms against any claim by his opponents to have created a social system embodying utopia on earth; but he has his own vision of an ordered society—never perfect—derived from his understanding of what man is, namely a being who needs to live with a sense of belonging in a world stable enough to be comprehensible.

We have no theory which does more than hint at the complexities involved, but we know a community when we see one, whether it be a village, a college, a group of friends, a collection of streets united by neighbourhood feeling, or a firm. Barchester was a community, the House of Commons, for all its fire and brimstone, is a community, Baldwin's old company was a community :

'It was a place where I knew and had known from childhood, every man on the ground; a place where I was able to talk with the men not only about the troubles in the works, but troubles at home and their wives. It was a place where strikes and lock-outs were unknown. It was a place where the fathers and grandfathers of the men then working there had worked, and where their sons went automatically to the business. It was also a place where nobody ever "got the sack" and where we had a natural

sympathy for those who were less concerned in efficiency than
is this generation, and where a large number of old gentlemen
used to spend their days sitting on the handles of wheel-barrows,
smoking their pipes."[1]

That is the sort of place in which most people want to work,
even if many may now prefer a co-operative board to family
ownership.

Is this nostalgia and idealism run riot? Well, yes, it is. The
purpose is to show that we too on the Conservative side have
some emotions to stir, and emotions much more conducive to
human happiness than the blood and mysticism of Marxism, or
the glittering prizes and sudden quicksands of Liberalism. Lest,
however, it is thought that the argument has wandered altogether
too far towards imaginary pastoral bliss, let us apply the Conservative approach to some areas which, we have predicted will
face us with increasingly desperate problems in the years ahead :
the problems of incomes policy, of industrial dereliction and of
the cities. There are plenty of others, such as the question of how
to manage, or replace, the nearly collapsing bureaucracy of the
National Health Service, which we could have discussed in this
section; the problems raised are meant to be examples, not an
exhaustive list. We will then end with a summary of the
approach, which, we believe, can offer the Conservative Party
a future to fight for, and a philosophy of living with which to
fight for it.

---

[1] Baldwin, speaking in 1925, quoted in Keith Middlemass and John Barnes,
Baldwin, (Weidenfeld and Nicolson 1969), p. 9.

PART IV

Policy

CHAPTER ONE

A Conservative Approach to Incomes Policy

When we discussed the events of the winter of 1973–4, we mentioned the dangers of the Liberal interpretation—that no government leadership of wages is possible at all. There followed also, in the second election of 1974 and subsequently, another misinterpretation, equally understandable but equally wrong. This view was naturally made the centrepiece of the propaganda of a Labour Party astonished at its own return to power, that the only way of maintaining any stability or any limitation on the demands of Trades Unionists was for the Labour Party to govern explicitly in the latter's interest and thereby buy industrial peace and some measure of incomes restraint. This view will turn out to be as ephemeral as the Liberal triumph in convincing some Conservatives that they should opt out of any attempt at leadership at all.

In the long term, its effect will be to further the organisation of other groups so as to form counterweights to the traditional unions (which will anyway decline). In the short term it will become apparent first, that the socialist price—of more nationalisation, bigger government and so higher taxes, and sympathy for Soviet Russia—is of little interest to most Trades Unionists concerned with job security, take home pay, immigration, and bad schools.

Second, the price exacted from the Government by the architects of this 'social contract' (socialist speech writers as usual borrow Liberal rhetoric to dress up their theories acceptably) is not a coherent programme : the expansion of government, the intimidation of private enterprise and the pouring of subsidies into non-productive industries produced between 1974 and 1977 the usual Labour Party high unemployment, to add to that which was anyway likely to follow the oil and commodity price rises of 1973-4, and the usual Labour Party overseas borrowing from capitalist lenders, ending in the usual Labour Party acceptance of very conservative financial policies dictated by the foreign lenders. The social contract has delivered few goods, and the first public sector strike of any significance against the Labour Government will turn the question 'will Trades Unions work with a Conservative Government?' into a political curio like Churchill's claim in 1946 that a Labour Government would mean a Gestapo in Britain, or Labour's that a Conservative Government in 1951 would mean a return to the conditions of the 1930s.

But what should the Conservative approach to incomes policy be? We have argued already that a statutory policy is impracticable. In part this is because of the necessary inflexibility of the law; the corollary is that the institutions and tactics of incomes leadership should vary according to the nature of the situation. But in one respect there is a general principle to follow. The need for incomes leadership stems from the fact that in nationalised industries (and in some cases in private industry where workers have been told that governments will not allow their firm to collapse—say, for reasons of national defence, like Rolls Royce) people do not believe the argument 'If we pay you this the company will go bust.' They do not believe it, not because they are wicked or stupid, but because it is false.

In nationalised industries, most of which have had immense debt written off by governments, all of which have access to Treasury finance, and in whose very statutes their existence in trust for the public is proclaimed, it is always artificial to try to pretend that the situation is the same as that in a private company. In a private company you can open the books and say: this is what we need for materials, this is what we have contracted to pay those who lent us the cash to start up operations or to expand, this is what we need to put aside for replacement of worn out equipment, this is the reserve we need for emergencies—and this (plus or minus the odd percent, about which negotiation can be genuine) is what is available for pay. In a nationalised industry, or a part of the government service, there is no such comprehensible self-contained system, of the functioning of which even the unwilling can in the end see the purpose. This is one very good reason for having as few nationalised industries and government bureaucracies as possible. For all that *their* managements have to offer in the way of unavoidable reality is a budgetary limit, or a Parliamentary vote— and everyone knows that budgets can be increased, and Parliamentary votes overturned.

So it is necessary to seek from workers in the nationalised industries understanding of the wider context of their demands— namely, what the *country* can afford. We must be able to say, and display the figures clearly to demonstrate, what lies behind the Treasury budget or the Parliamentary vote. Virtually nothing has been done in this direction yet. Such pay norms as have been negotiated, Mr Selwyn Lloyd's, Mr Barber's, Mr Healey's and the others, have been handed down from the Treasury *ex cathedra*. The best, as usual, is the enemy of the good : because no simple economic balance-sheet will win the assent of every econometrician, we have to put up with a situation where the Chancellor's assertions, backed by nothing popularly comprehensible whatever, are to be taken simply on trust by the public. It is greatly to the latter's credit that it has gone along as well as it has. But in fact it *is* possible to derive a figure, sensible, but not, of course, exact, of what would be available on different assumptions about the future for wages, of what would be the consequences in prices and unemployment if that figure was seriously breached, and of what freedom of action in terms of taxation could follow its achievement. Such an approach allows also instant, and comprehensible, corrective action if some major change in one of the important variables outside Britain's control should occur, as was the case with commodity and oil prices in 1972–4.

Mr Healey has moved some way towards such a system by his linking of pay levels to income tax cuts : there is nothing at all wicked or stupid in such a recognition that voluntary social discipline can lessen the extent of necessary government coercion. He may be criticised for the piece-meal approach, for talking only to a few Trades Unionists, and above all for not displaying more than the hem of the petticoat of Treasury thinking about the future : but not for making a commonsense connection between pay restraint and other variables in the economy.

Once such a figure has been derived, then it should be possible much more explicitly to formalise and greatly to widen the

process of discussion aimed at securing consent to it and understanding of it. It will not much matter if no firm agreement is
signed; if at the end of the discussions, a figure of 5% or 6% for
that year is generally accepted as what is feasible, the climate will
have been enormously influenced. Some private industries, opening the books and showing a tight situation, may get away with
2%; some workers may insist on 12% as a result of new profits,
though government pressure would be for the reinvestment of the
fruits of such success and the creation of more, slightly less
lucrative jobs. Some will break the norm : in the private sector
they will suffer the consequences and people will be better placed
to understand why. In the public sector, no new weapons will
be available, other than those which now exist of restraint on
future investments, the seeking of alternative sources of supply,
and ultimately restraint on the economy as a whole—but a long
course of discussion, education and negotiation will have been
navigated before the point of confrontation of government and
other workers by such a recalcitrant group in the public sector
is reached.

A further use of any forum for national pay discussion, along
one of the various lines suggested by Lord Brown, Professor
Meade[1] and others, would be in clarifying the truth that, since
reality cannot be altered, those who make excessive claims take
either from investment for the future or from other workers. This
in itself would be useful.

There is nothing new in such proposals. Nor are they a panacea, nor a substitute for skilful government and strong leadership.
An effective government will always need its Sir Walter
Monckton or its Sir Jack Scamp if it is to succeed. They do however derive from an approach to society which is Conservative in
the sense we have described it. People will only behave in a co-
operative way if their behaviour is part of the working of a
comprehensible community—that is, if they recognise something
in which to co-operate. Private firms, co-operatively run in the
broadest sense (and sometimes in the technical sense) can form
such communities because their working is easy to explain and
the effects of different courses of action predictable. In the
nationalised industries, and large State bureaucracies, it is

---

[1] See Bibliography.

extremely difficult to point to the existence of such an explicable community, other than that based on propositions like 'we are all in it (the mines, railways, Inland Revenue) together and had better look after ourselves'. Therefore, if these latter organisations cannot be dissolved (which they cannot) the strength of the national community must be called into use to right the balance. And that means an all-pervasive attempt to show how that national community, in its financial aspect, works. The attempt has never yet seriously been made. Conservatives should welcome the chance to be the first to try.

CHAPTER TWO

Industrial and Urban Dereliction: A Conservative Approach

1. *A New Approach to Regional Policy.*

Very considerable areas of Britain, once proud centres of man-ufacturing and exporting industries, have now declined to the point where even in good times their unemployment is twice or three times the national average—and that after the creation of much subsidised employment which exists only so long as richer regions of the country put up with it. The oldest and most famous of these areas are in Northern Ireland, Scotland, on Merseyside and in the North East; but there are plenty of young people out of work in say, South London or Southampton who prove that the whole of Southern England is not prosper-ous.

What is more, there are depressing signs of industrial weak-ness in even the stronger regions; in every recession the industrial base of the country becomes weaker as the number of home suppliers of some critical component drop from half a dozen to one or two—who may then disappear altogether, making some vital industry dependent on imports. It is easy for macro-economic experts and others who deal only in aggregates to think of industry as some massive, monolithic whole, a great machine which can be stopped or started at will. It is not so : some White-hall mandarins might be astonished at the tenuousness of some of the vital links in the chain of supply. If the whole process is jerked to a stop, some of these snap, each time : some small specialist firms just go out of production, or suffer damage from which they never recover, or get so undercut by cheap imports available for the purpose of market penetration, that they cannot compete. So our industrial base becomes smaller, so we are driven out of home production in yet another basic product—while at the same time our total national 'overhead' is steadily increased by the various pressures on the political process at which we looked earlier.

The result, as magisterially described by Bacon and Eltis,[1] is a Britain with too few producers or, at least, too few working with the level of productivity necessary to maintain the standard of life apparently promised by the political process. Meanwhile the whittling away of industry under the relentless competition of the outside world and the direct effect this has on people's lives is quite beyond the ken of those who work in the bureaucracy. They are used to failure and retreat—are now so used to it that they can often imagine nothing else—but theirs is a different world, where retreat means expansion in terms of jobs, pay and status: there are far more permanent under-secretaries in Whitehall failing to deal with the problems of fifty-five millions in the United Kingdom than there were coping with—what was it?—a fifth of the world's population scattered over thousands of miles threequarters of a century ago.

This is not something for which civil servants can particularly be blamed—they are simply the beneficiaries of the trend towards bigger government, even if they have been zealous somewhat beyond the call of duty in advancing their own pay and pensions at the expense of others. But their different experience—their security, their natural tendency to think that the model of every organisation is that of the government bureaucracy, their suspicion of monetary gain (non-salaried monetary gain, that is) as a motive for action, their lack of understanding of the interrelationship between action and persuasion ('that's Parliament's job, old man')—all conspire to make government bureaucracies, even adorned by a few industrial luminaries, normally of the recently retired variety grouped in advisory committees, singularly unsuitable creatures for the regeneration of industry.

There is little hope that sectoral plans, National Economic Development Council strategies, initiatives by Departments, pronouncements by Ministers (especially before elections), or centrally planned regional policies, will ever much affect the world; they will keep some thousands in subsidised jobs, both in 'industry' and in the controlling bureaucracy, but they will not change the economic climate on Merseyside or in Glasgow.

Perhaps the truth is that, in the face of the movement against

[1] Op. cit.

us of world industrial trends, nothing will succeed. But before we come to such gloomy conclusions we have to make a more serious attempt than anything the poor Department of Industry can manage. A Conservative approach will not fear throwing the weight of the State into the scales. Indeed, if Conservatives come to the conclusion, as in most of the regions we are talking about it is reasonable to conclude, that capital and jobs will not return by themselves, then the State will be abdicating responsibility if it does nothing. It cannot condemn those of its citizens who happen to be born in the relevant areas to a permanent twilight world of subsidy, decline, and decay; nor will the rest of the country for ever be able to waste such surplus as it generates by pouring it into the sand in this way. Such a course—what may be called the 'present policy' course—is almost *designed* to foster extremist politics in both declining and prosperous regions by pitting the one against the other; and its long term consequences will be futile.

The principles on which a new policy must be based are these. First, without a regeneration of the spirit of people working—or not working—in the relevant area, money spent on building factories or staving off bankruptcies is money down the drain. There will be various ways of attempting this regeneration. Sometimes there will be a genuine industrial leader—a man who can command loyalties and carry through hard decisions—who can be called in aid, and who must be given freedom of action in the way no bureaucrat will like. Sometimes the way forward will be that which has been muddied by Mr Wedgwood Benn's ill-judged experiments—via co-operatives. The latter is likely to be a route about which we must be much braver. Everyone extols the virtue of the small firm, and the partnership—rightly, because such units are small enough to allow the understanding of what is happening and the mutual trust of a face-to-face community to operate. Co-operatives (of which there are anyway multifarious different sorts) are one way, by no means the only way, of getting back from a situation of dereliction towards one where people understand what must be done, and why. Why should Conservatives be so frightened of such self-regulating communities, when rural and small-town existence is at the heart of their tradition? Of course there must be authority in such co-operatives, and of course every decision cannot be taken by the vote;

but if such truths have been forgotten, self-education in them is one way forward. It would be far better to give the bankrupt shipyards to the workers in them, to let them propose a plan for the necessary abolition of demarcation problems and the rest, than to set up a mammoth centralised bureaucracy, run by retired civil servants, politicians, and admirals from the list of the Great and the Good, as if shipbuilding was a social service or a government department. But the latter course, followed by the Labour Government, will ensure, if anything can, that before long shipbuilding in Britain will, in fact, be indistinguishable from a branch of the social services.

All this implies that the government's role should be to provide finance only where there are people to finance. It will be very difficult. It will not be possible to be even handed : if movements of regeneration start in Scotland, the money should go to Scotland, because then there is a chance that it will not be wasted, and not to another region where it will disappear. Of course, a background of income-support must be afforded across the board, but discretionary aid must be truly discretionary to be any use. There will be mistakes, some corruption, and waste. Wrong judgements will be made. But the attempt to distribute every penny in an even handed way, with accountability as strict as if the expenditure was still inside the bureaucracy (which admittedly, nowadays, is not as strict as all that) will simply mean that *all* the money is wasted. I am deliberately steering clear of institutions in arguing for an approach. But the approach obviously implies a regional policy dominated not by the London departments and initiated not by their local out-stations, but in the hands of those in the regions. The funnel through which state aid goes is always the problem. Local government is not the correct medium : its instincts are no closer to industry than those of central government. Perhaps a resident Cabinet Minister with his own council of advisers should be assigned to a region : against the chaos of near civil war, the way in which some new industry has been generated in Ulster has been instructive.

2. *Tariffs.*
Throughout, it is the finding, or the creating, of the functioning community at work which is the *sine qua non* of success. If

some success is achieved, no government should hesitate for a moment to use protective tariffs to guard against the counter-attacks which could be expected from overseas competitors. No one who has studied the growth of industry in Germany, America or Japan, or who watches what is now happening in newly industrialising countries, or who appreciates the unfair advantages which financial and imperial strength gave Britain in the brief period of nineteenth century free trade—or even the relative success derived from continuing the McKenna tariffs after the First World War—can doubt that protection must have its place in any successful launching or relaunching of new industries.

3. *Incentives*

It is, however, undoubtedly true, as economic Liberals have claimed, that the process of erosion of incentives necessary to allow the free-enterprise sector of industry to function effectively, must be reversed. At present, Britain is well on the way to being a society without the monetary rewards necessary for free enterprise, and yet without a majority in favour of a centrally-directed economy which would be, at least, one alternative.[2] The foolish tinkering with indirect tax rates, together with the dubiously legal use of inflation to carry more people every year into ever higher rates of direct tax, must be reversed. Such a reversal will not provide a panacea of itself : a miraculous new enthusiasm for work will not overnight improve Britain's underlying growth rate. The belief that it might is yet another failed growthmanship policy. But it must be absurd for the government of a country which is not fundamentally wealthy so to abuse the tax system that its basic principle becomes not that the better-off should contribute to the poor, but that unusual achievement should be penalised. Such half-way egalitarianism merely sabotages one kind of work-ethic without providing anything in its place—just as special taxes on savings penalise individual savers while the proponents of such taxation lack anything to offer in their necessary place.

Conservatives indeed believe that financial gain is the *sole*

---

[2] As a matter of fact, there is a good deal of evidence that even centrally-directed economies, such as Russia and China, find it convenient to have wider differences between pay after tax, than do the British in 1977.

motivation of few in a sound society; but it is one sensible motivator, much preferable to the direction of labour and savings which is its most obvious alternative. Inequalities of income and of wealth must be limited on the one side by a judgement of the excesses which will break a community by providing an individual with intolerable advantages, and on the other by the fact that in very nearly all (though not quite all) of the communities in which people live successfully it is readily agreed that free competition for rewards which it becomes the winner's right to keep is the best way of carrying out many tasks of economic life.

Conservatives in Britain now can be at one with Liberals in their belief that an explicit widening of inequalities (differentials is the respectable word, hallowed by Trades Union use) is necessary if the economy is to continue to work at all. Conservatives will sympathise both with craft unions' desire for the status inherent in valuable work to be reflected in a status element in pay, and with the Liberals' desire for the restoration of some closer relation between pay and the value of the product. On the one hand, the static hierarchy of the Trades Unionist strikes a nostalgic chord reminiscent of the harking back to feudalism of early Conservatives. On the other the Liberals' supposedly self-adjusting economic machine helps Conservatives to restrain the growth of the State. But neither is the whole story. The Conservative approach is to believe that all such total theories imply the magnification of partial insights or single genuine observations into grand theory—at once dangerous and false. But to say that more will be needed than the restoration of incentives, better rewards for achievement, and encouragement for savers, if we are to succeed as a nation, is not to say that those things are not necessary. The clearance of some of the debris of dead social democracy will be necessary for those who succeed it, whether Conservative or Marxist.

4. *The Part-Time Work Society.*

Such a new approach to industrial policy against the background of the restoration of more generally acceptable rewards for work would pay some dividends. But in the long term, as we have argued it is likely that even a successful policy will never provide as many industrial jobs in Britain as we would like. We will need the fall in population that we seem now to be getting. That will imply strict controls against the increasing pressures of immigration. It will imply a difficult period of readjustment when there is an ageing population, carried by the declining work-force which may already be expected from the late 1980s onwards. Life expectancy will increase somewhat more, though the scientific advances which will allow greatly increased longevity are probably still some way off—and will be very expensive (posing great problems of allocation) when they first arrive. But the problems of a smaller work force in the age range 16–65, a larger population over 65 (somewhat balanced after the early 1980s by a smaller one under 16) will pose considerable questions for the way in which work and total income are distributed.

We will have the choice between letting a few generate the wealth at work, and an expanding government machine distribute it to the many who will not be producing anything saleable; or, on the other hand, letting more share in work and in the wealth they themselves help to create. To a Conservative, already concerned about the expansion of the State, the latter is much the preferable course. A future of work-sharing—a world where the part-time job in industry, or perhaps intermittent full time periods at work organised in a predictable way, is normal—should hold no terrors for Conservatives who will welcome the time thus available again for the citizen to involve himself in his local community and in the development of such private skills as he may have. Great benefit could come also from the ending of the watershed break of retirement when men or women go out of work with the clear implication that society merely awaits their death. The part-time work society could be much more flexible, with profit to human dignity. That it will be a world more difficult for Trades Unions to dominate is no disadvantage either: though in the first instance, people are likely increasingly to join unions as a form of protective insurance, the world of part-time work is likely later to see a rapid growth in the non-unionised self-employed.

These longer-term projections depend on our so ordering our affairs that relatively capital intensive industries, worked by relatively few, generate sufficient surplus for such a standard of life. It may be that we do not so order our affairs. Then what will happen will be less pleasant : we will all work, but the return for our work will be nearer and nearer to subsistence. The outcome, of course, will be somewhere in between : neither industrial aristocrats, nor industrial serfs—but pockets of each, and mixtures of both. It is with subjects such as these that the next governments of Britain will have to grapple.

5. *Cities.*

Gloomy prognostications about many of our big cities are hard to avoid, for the reasons given in pages 18 to 19. Unemployment, physical decay of the buildings, parks and roads, loss of amenities, racial tension, will all continue to follow the decline of those traditional industries which surround most large towns—and these problems may be very persistent if we are right in predicting a long-term transference of wealth to newly industrialising nations and to our own countryside as food scarcities increase world-wide. How should Conservatives face the problem of the cities?

First, we should stand appalled at what has been done, often by Conservative governments and local councils, in the physical destruction of our cities in the last thirty years. Nothing has been safe. Even Oxford, even Bath—unique world treasures with which even the most magnificent picture or even the most splendid country houses are not to be compared—have been vandalised. The pressure has been unremitting, and continues. A battle won can be reopened when the clamour has subsided. We have one of the worst records in the civilised world for the preservation of our finest citites; and this failure is matched by proportionate failures down the scale to preserve ordinary towns as functioning communities. It is not just that we have cleared and rebuilt shoddily at the dictates of a dead social science which thought it could 'build an environment' better than the community itself. We have *kept* clearing and rebuilding; there is no end to it. New roads where cars should not be, pointless housing estates when city-centres are empty, barbarous private fashions in the architectural world. The last generation of town planners should hang their heads in shame. Their grandchildren will, on their behalf.

Terrible damage has been done by the proponents of 'modernism' in architecture who over-rode centuries of subtle tradition with shoddy theories whose intellectual poverty we can all see and judge, made manifest in concrete and steel. Somehow, because in the English tradition architects have been respected men—as well they might be with Wren and Vanbrugh as their exemplars—no one could quite believe that the remaining proponents of the totalitarian architecture of the 1920s and 1930s in Europe, operating in Britain, were not fine fellows who should be given knighthoods. Some were, like Pevsner and Martin. In fact, they were as pernicious a collection as the vulgarisers of Marx whom they resemble. On the whole, the establishment resisted the latter more effectively.[3]

The tide seems to have turned now. How should a Conservative set about strengthening the powers available to a community to frustrate those who childishly think that the District Council Planning Department will be able to build a better city than has been evolved over a thousand years, or to foil those who stand to make money in the process? We must do to the planning process something akin to what we have to do to the constitution: protect it from the activist, the possessor of the grand theory, the final solution. Make compulsory purchase *more* difficult, not less—not so much on Liberal grounds that private property is a natural, inalienable right (it is possible to imagine a satisfactory society without it) but because private property plus plenty of appeal courts is one very good way of limiting the dangers of planning. Let us have local referendums

---

[3] David Watkin, in an excellent little book, *Morality and Architecture*, (Oxford, 1977) demonstrates the disastrous influence of grand theorists on architecture in Britain from Pugin's *Contrasts* in 1836 to Pevsner's *Pioneers of the Modern Movement* in 1936. A quotation from the latter gives the flavour of the book.

'For various reasons England forfeited her leadership in the shaping of the new style just after 1900, that is, at the very moment when the work of all the pioneers began to converge into one universal movement. One reason was . . . the levelling tendency of the coming mass movement—and a true architectural style *is* a mass movement—was too much against the grain of the English character. A similar antipathy prevented the ruthless scrapping of traditions which was essential to the achievement of a style fitting our century' (p. 165–6). Pevsner repeatedly argues that a 'genuine style' must be totalitarian, and that individualism is to be regarded as an unsatisfactory deviation. Many thousands of people will live for years to come in the sterile and inhuman environment this doctrine produced.

on major projects. Let us have laws which compel access by interested local groups into the pre-planning of local authorities —who are often even more secretive than central government. Let us have council houses and flats given at much reduced prices to long standing tenants, so that, freed from the patronising feudal arrangements of council tenancy, new armies of owner occupiers may be added to those with access to newly strengthened powers of opposition to grand local planning. Such enfranchised council-tenants would then for the first time have the chance to start creating the sense of free standing community which no tenancy, especially under council conditions, can give. A greater distribution of real wealth, and a greater limitation of central bureaucracy, would follow from such a policy than from almost any other.

In short, if as Conservatives we believe in the social and moral importance of community, we must look to the preservation of the physical landmarks without which no community is possible. We should propose a new charter to protect the citizen from the physical planners. Give buildings to groups of people to renovate themselves; fear general clearance like the plague which it resembles, and restore and renovate even if the short term costs are higher—the long term costs of doing it wrong will not appear in the planners' balance sheet, since they include such things as the cost of Detention Centres for juvenile criminals. Consult, call for votes, hold referendums—interest people in the alternatives, and do not worry about the chaos caused thereby to bureaucratic decision matrices. If the people are not committed to what is done, you are wasting the government's money anyway. Many people *want* to live in cities, if they are given the chance; it is a unique achievement of our particular culture at the moment to make them flee from Georgian terraces, Victorian parks, twentieth-century cinemas, and all the inducements of the pleasanter side of town life. But no one can live in a city which increasingly resembles a half-built airport interspersed with unreclaimed bomb sites. Here is a programme for Conservatives: to conserve city life. If we could achieve that, we need not worry about the electoral map being blue where there are more cows than people, and red where the ratio is reversed.

PART V

Conclusion
The Conservative Tradition

The Conservative Tradition

If a political philosophy is to be of any use to a party, it must do three things. First it must provide, in however hazy a form, an idea, of a kind from which effective slogans can be derived, towards which those who work for the party's success can struggle, and, believing in which, they can withstand the pressures and frustration of the democratic competition. The socialist's cry of equality and his vision (extremely vague) of a society embodying it; the Liberal's liberty, with its lawless utopia; are both in their way powerful and successful attempts to fill this need : they gather together ever present innate drives—their opponents would say the drives of envy and of selfishness respectively—and use them for idealised ends.

Second, a practical political approach in a democratic world must offer the chance of attracting enough of the different groups and interests in the nation to give a hope of power. An approach so unrealistic that serious compromises with its basic tenets are inevitably part of the tactics necessary to bring the believers to power cannot survive for long unless it overturns the democratic process. Neither socialist nor Liberal have succeeded very well in this respect—both attaching themselves, by their very nature, to specific minority interests in the nation, defined in terms of the classes of classical economic or Marxist theory.

Third, and perhaps most often forgotten, a party must have a philosophy of government which will guide it when it gains office—if it is not simply to accept whatever fashion is current amongst its advisers. If Ministers think they can avoid theory by appeal to common sense, they should remember the words of Maynard Keynes :

'Practical men who believe themselves quite exempt from any intellectual influences, are usually the slaves of some defunct

F

economist. Madmen in authority, who hear voices in the air, are distilling their frenzy from some academic scribbler of a few years back.'[1]

It is one of the arguments of this book that Liberalism now provides no useful map across the political landscape for the Minister in power, other than to tell him what he could do if the mountains were plains and the swamps navigable rivers; that the two 'moderate' philosophies of Social Democracy and Keynesian Conservatism, predicated as they are on being able to deliver an impossibly regular growth, and on allowing steady increase of government which they cannot then administer, are philosophies based on fundamental contradictions which cannot survive in a world of shortages and of popular reaction against bureaucracy; and that the only remaining alternative to Conservatism, Marxism, is nonsense and mysticism dressed up as respectable argument, providing all the necessary self-justification for tyranny of the worst sort.

An attempt has here been made to argue that the Conservative tradition promises a sensible future for its adherents on all these fronts.

Its vision is of a world stable enough to allow people to develop to the full in the only circumstances in which the human animal can so do—in communities, for living, at work, at play, on a human scale. A sound society based around such multifarious natural groups—villages, small towns, properly organised places of work, localities of cities—will contain sufficient variety to ward off the Conservative's nightmare : the imposition of some all-embracing theory of the organisation of society. The attempt permanently to establish such a theory the Conservative regards as intellectually disreputable and, in political terms, a sure road to tyranny or anarchy.

The Conservative knows that the role of the independent, arbitrating State must be a supreme one, free from the control of any one group or community, and acting where necessary to prevent abuse and right a balance, while leaving to the communities of the nation as much of their self-regulation as is possible. He understands, too, that the State will win no allegiance if it steps outside its proper role.

[1] J. M. Keynes, *The General Theory of Employment, Interest, and Money*, (Macmillan, London, 1936) p. 383.

The Conservative understands that the basic moral values are assumptions lying behind any social or political propositions, and not derivable from the latter. Some will say they are God-given; others that they inhere in the nature of man, and that though they may change slowly over millenia, and though few will agree exactly on any exhaustive catalogue of things which are right and wrong without question, few will argue about a central list which turns up regularly wherever civilised life lasts.

The Conservative is therefore not much impressed with arguments derived from fashionable social or political theory which say that the State—or anyone else—must refrain from taking action to right a wrong, because some book says that that wrong is a necessary wrong.

Ours is the *only* philosophy which does not seek to turn people against one another—but to use as the test of whatever issue is currently pressing, say, income-distribution or education, the question 'which arrangement will best help to preserve the complex honeycomb of society, with all its interdependencies?' If it links this feeling for the whole, for the community, with a robust defence against the desecration of such actual communities as are threatened by the theorists, it will find itself gathering electoral support from town and country in a way which will dispense with electoral worries.

Finally, Conservatism is a philosophy of government which will not leave its leaders intellectually naked in the Cabinet Room. At a time when society is nearly shattered, when increasingly powerless and increasingly desperate solitary citizens face the rambling structure of an ever-expanding State which can reach out and turn their lives upside down for the most trivial and unpredictable reasons, Conservative governments must seek to bring back the role of the State within its proper limits and to assist in every way the nurture of the necessary communities in which alienated individuals can live. There is a consistent programme, both of limitation and of nurturing, some of the principles for which are discussed in this book, and much of the practical politics of which is embedded in the current programme of the Conservative Party.

History is on our side. Once again, as apparently all-conquering political fashions crumble away after short years of arrogant dominance, basic Conservative truths quietly emerge from hiding. We have ahead of us the dangerous period of the apparent triumph—but in reality the imminent collapse—of Marxist-Leninism, of its Western disciples, and of its Russian Empire. When both Marx and Lenin are of interest only to historians and antiquarians, when the Russian Empire follows the Roman, the Spanish, and the British into the sunset, Conservatism—the philosophy of man in his community—will still be vigorous. And in the years immediately ahead, Britain can be thankful that it has a party which, by and large, sometimes more effectively and sometimes less, gives that philosophy lasting embodiment.

Bibliography

The editions cited are those which I found most immediately accessible. In some cases they are not the latest available.

Albrow, Martin, *Bureaucracy*, London, 1970

Amery, Leo, *Conservatism—Chambers Encyclopaedia*, London, 1950

Amery, Leo, *Thoughts on the Constitution*, London, 1953

Aristotle, *Ethica Nichomachea*, ed. L. Bywater, Oxford, 1962

Aristotle, *Politica*, ed. W. D. Ross, Oxford, 1957

Arrow, Kenneth J., *Social Choice and Individual Values*, Second edition, London, 1963

Bacon, Robert and Eltis, Walter, *Britain's Economic Problem: Too Few Producers*, London, 1976

Bagehot, Walter, *The English Constitution*, Introd. R. H. S. Crossman, London, 1963

Bagehot, Walter, *Historical Essays*, Introd. N. St. John-Stevas, New York, 1965

Barker, Sir Ernest (ed), *Social Contract*, London, 1947

Barry, Brian, *The Liberal Theory of Justice: A Critical Examination of the Principal Doctrines in 'A Theory of Justice' by John Rawls*, Oxford, 1973

Beer, Samuel H., *British Politics in the Collectivist Age*, New York, 1969

Beer, Samuel H. and Ulam, Adam (eds), *Patterns of Government*, New York, 1962

Bell, Daniel, *The End of Ideology: On The Exhaustion of Political Ideas in The Fifties*, New York, 1960

Bellairs, Charles E., *Conservative Social and Industrial Reform: A Record of Conservative Legislation between 1800 and 1974*, London, 1977

Bentinck, Lord Henry, *Tory Democracy*, London, 1918

Berlin, Sir Isaiah, *Four Essays on Liberty*, Oxford, 1969

Berlin, Sir Isaiah, *The Hedgehog and the Fox*, London, 1953

Blake, Robert (Lord Blake), *The Conservative Party From Peel to Churchill*, London, 1970

Blake, Robert and Patten, John (eds), *The Conservative Opportunity*, London, 1976

Bolingbroke, Henry St John, Viscount, *On The Idea of a Patriot King*, London, 1775

Boswell, James, *Life of Dr Johnson* (2 Vols.), London, 1958

Brewster, Sir David, *Memoirs of Newton* (2 Vols.), London, 1855

Brittan, Samuel, *Left or Right: The Bogus Dilemma*, London, 1968

Brittan, Samuel, *Steering the Economy: The Role of the Treasury*, London, 1969

Brittan, Samuel, *Capitalism and The Permissive Society*, London, 1973

Brittan, Samuel, *Is There an Economic Consensus?*, London, 1973

Brittan, Samuel, *Second Thoughts on Full Employment Policy*, London, 1975

Brown, Wilfred (Lord Brown), *The Earnings Conflict*, London, 1973

Bruce-Gardyne, Jock and Lawson, Nigel, *The Power Game: an Examination of Decision Making in Government*, London, 1976

Burke, Edmund, *Speeches and Letters on American Affairs, and Speech to the Electors of Bristol*, London, 1956

Burke, Edmund, *Reflections on the Revolution in France*, London, 1960

Butler, David and Stokes, Donald, *Political Change in Britain: Forces Shaping Electoral Choice*, London, 1969

Cecil, Lord Hugh, *Conservatism*, London, 1912

Centre for Agricultural Strategy, *Land for Agriculture*, Reading, 1976

Coleraine, Lord, *For Conservatives Only*, London, 1970

Coleridge, Samuel Taylor, *On the Constitution of the Church and State*, London, 1972

Conservative Party Manifesto, 1970, *A Better Tomorrow, The Conservative Programme for the next Five Years*, London, 1970

Crosland, C. A. R., *The Future of Socialism*, London, 1956

Crossman, Richard, *Inside View*, London, 1972

Deutsch, Karl W., *Nationalism and Social Communication: an Enquiry into the Foundations of Nationality*, Cambridge, Mass., 1953

Deutsch, Karl W., *The Nerves of Government: Models of Political Communication and Control*, New York, 1963

Diels, Hermann and Kranz, Walther, *Die Fragmente der Vorsokratiker*, Zurich/Berlin, 1964

Durkheim, E., *Suicide, a Study in Sociology*, Trans. J. A. Spaulding and G. Simpson, London, 1952

Dworkin, Ronald, *The Original Position,* in University of Chicago Law Review, Vol. 40, Number 3, Spring 1973

Eliot, T. S., *Notes Towards the Definition of Culture,* London, 1948

Expenditure Committee of the House of Commons, Eleventh Report, London, 1977

Finer, S. E. (ed.), *Adversary Politics and Electoral Reform,* London, 1975

Fitzgerald, F. Scott, *Tender is the Night,* London, 1953

Friedman, Milton, *Capitalism and Freedom,* Chicago, 1962

Friedman, Milton, *An Economist's Protest,* New Jersey, 1972

Friedrich, Carl J., *Tradition and Authority,* London, 1972

Frye, Northrop, *The Stubborn Structure: Essays on Criticism and Society,* London, 1970

Gamble, Andrew, *The Conservative Nation,* Routledge, 1974

Gash, Norman, *Peel,* London, 1975

Gilmour, Sir Ian, *The Body Politic,* London, 1969

Gilmour, Sir Ian, *Inside Right: A Study of Conservatism,* London, 1977

Grant, Michael, *Roman History from Coins,* Cambridge, 1958

Guttman, W. and Meehan, P., *The Great Inflation, Germany 1919–23,* Farnborough, 1975

Haines, Joe, *The Politics of Power,* London, 1977

Hanson, A. H., *Planning and the Politicians and Other Essays,* London, 1968

Hare, R. M., *Rawl's Theory of Justice,* Philosophical Quarterly, p. 144–55, and p. 247–52, 1973

Harris, Nigel, *Competition and the Corporate Society: British Conservatives, the State and Industry, 1945–64,* London, 1972

Harris, Ralph and Sewill, Brendan, *British Economic Policy 1970–74: Two Views,* London, 1975

Harris, Ralph and Seldon, Arthur, *Not from Benevolence . . . Twenty Years of Economic Dissent,* London, 1977

Hart, H. L. A., *The Concept of Law,* Oxford, 1961

Hayek, F. A. Von, *The Road to Serfdom,* London, 1944

Hayek, F. A. Von, *Economic Freedom and Representative Government,* London, 1973

Hayek, F. A. Von, *Law Legislation and Liberty* (Vol. I), London, 1973

Hayek, F. A. Von, *Law, Legislation and Liberty* (Vol. II), London, 1976

Hecclo, H. and Wildavsky, A., *The Private Government of Public Money,* London, 1973

Heimann, Eduard, *History of Economic Doctrines,* Oxford, 1972

Hegel, G. W. F., *Phenomenology of Spirit*, Trans. A. V. Miller, Oxford, 1977

Hegel, G. W. F., *Philosophy of Right*, Trans. R. M. Knox, Oxford, 1967

Hirsch, Fred, *Social Limits to Growth*, London, 1977

Hobbes, Thomas, *Leviathan*, Oxford, 1965

Hogg, Quintin (Lord Hailsham), *The Conservative Case*, London, 1959

Hogg, Quintin (Lord Hailsham), *The Door Wherein I Went*, London, 1975

Hogg, Quintin (Lord Hailsham), *Elective Dictatorship: The Dimbleby Lecture, 1976*, London, 1976

Hollis, Christopher, *The Crisis of Parliamentary Government*, The Cambridge Journal, Vol. I, 1947/8 p. 172–7

Hoyle, Sir Fred, *Energy or Extinction: The Case for Nuclear Energy*, London, 1977

Hume, David, *Dialogues Concerning Natural Religion*, New York, 1966

Hume, David, *A Treatise of Human Nature*, Dent, 1974

Jay, Peter, *Employment, Inflation and Politics*, London, 1963

Jay, Peter, *'Ending the Age of Full Employment'*, in *The Times*, April 10th, 1975

Jay, Peter, *'Tour des Cycles'*, in *The Times*, May 8th, 1975

Jenkins, Roy, *What Matters Now*, London, 1972

Jouvenal, Bertrand de, *Pure Theory of Politics*, London, 1963

Jouvenal, Bertrand de, *Sovereignty: An Enquiry into the Political Good*, London, 1957

Kahn, Herman, Brown, William and Martel, Leon, *The Next 200 Years*, London, 1977

Kant, Immanuel, *On History*, New York, 1963

Kavanagh, Dennis, *Political Culture*, London, 1972

Keynes, John Maynard, *The General Theory of Employment, Interest and Money*, London, 1936

Kirk, G. and Raven, J. E., *The Pre-Socratic Philosophers*, Cambridge, 1972

Kirk, Russell, *The Conservative Mind*, Chicago, 1969

Kolakowski, Leszek and Hampshire, Stuart (eds), *The Socialist Idea: A Reappraisal*, Reading, 1974

Lakatos, Imre and Musgrave, Alan (eds), *Criticism and the Growth of Knowledge*, Cambridge, 1970

Laslett, Peter, *The Face to Face Society*, p. 157–184 in *Philosophy, Politics and Society*, ed. P. Laslett, Oxford, 1956

Laslett, Peter, *The World We Have Lost*, London, 1975

Leach, Sir Edmund, *A Runaway World?*, Reith Lectures 1967, London, 1968

Lively, Jack, *Democracy*, Oxford, 1975

Locke, John, *Two Treatises of Government*, introd. P. Laslett, Cambridge, 1960

Lukes, Steven, *Alienation and Anomie*, in *Philosophy, Politics and Society*, Ed. P. Laslett and W. G. Runciman, Oxford, 1969

Machiavelli, Niccolo, *The Prince and the Discourses*, Ed. Max Lerner, New York, 1950

Macmillan, Harold, *The Middle Way*, London, 1938

Maistre, Joseph de, *Works*, ed. and trans. J. Lively, New York, 1965

Marcuse, Herbert, *Repressive Tolerance*, Boston, 1965

Marx, Karl, *The Early Texts*, ed. D. McLellan, Oxford, 1971

Marx, Karl, *Capital*, Vol. I, ed. Ernest Mandel, London, 1976

Marx, Karl and Engels, Friedrich (ed. Lewis S. Feuer), *Basic Writings on Politics and Philosophy*, New York, 1959

Marx, Karl and Engels, Friedrich, *Manifesto of the Communist Party*, Peking, 1975

Meade, James E., *The Intelligent Radical's Guide to Economic Policy*, London, 1975

Middlemass, Keith and Barnes, John, *Baldwin*, London, 1969

Mill, J. S., *On Liberty*, New York, 1956

Mishan, E. J., *The Economic Growth Debate: An Assessment*, London, 1977

Nagel, Thomas, *Rawls on Justice, Philosophical Review*, 1973, p. 220–34

Nisbet, Robert, *Twilight of Authority*, London, 1976

Nozick, Robert, *Anarchy, State and Utopia*, Oxford, 1974

Oakeshott, Michael, *Rationalism in Politics*, in *Cambridge Journal*, Vol. I, 1947/48 p. 81–98, 145–57

Oakeshott, Michael, *Contemporary British Politics* in *Cambridge Journal*, Vol. I, 1947/48 p. 474–90

Oakeshott, Michael, *Political Education*, p. 1–21 in *Philosophy, Politics and Society*, ed. P. Laslett, Oxford, 1956

Oakeshott, Michael, *On Human Conduct*, Oxford, 1975

Olson, Mancur, *The Logic of Collective Action: Public Goods and the Theory of Groups*, Cambridge, Mass, 1975

Orwell, George, *Animal Farm*, London, 1945

Pelling, Henry, *A History of British Trades Unionism*, London, 1963

Pevsner, Sir Nikolaus, *Pioneers of the Modern Movement*, London, 1936

Plamenatz, J. P., *Consent, Freedom and Political Obligation*, Oxford, 1968

Plant, Raymond, *Community and Ideology: An Essay in Applied Social Philosophy*, London, 1974

Plato, *Res Publica*, ed. J. Burnet, Oxford, 1965

Popper, K. R., *The Open Society and Its Enemies*, Vol. I, Plato. Vol. II, Hegel and Marx, London, 1962

Powell, Enoch, *A Nation not Afraid—The Thinking of Enoch Powell*, ed. J. Wood, London, 1965

Quinton, Anthony (ed), *Political Philosophy*, Oxford, 1971

Raison, Timothy, *Why Conservative?*, London, 1964

Rawls, John, *Justice as Fairness*, in *Philosophy, Politics and Society*, 2nd Series, ed. P. Laslett and W. G. Runciman, Oxford, 1962

Rawls, John, *A Theory of Justice*, Oxford, 1972

Report of the Committee of Inquiry on Industrial Democracy, Chairman, Lord Bullock Cmnd. 6706, London, 1977

Ricardo, David, *The Works and Correspondence*, ed. P. Sraffa and M. H. Dobb, Vol. I, *On The Principles of Political Economy and Taxation*, Cambridge, 1951

Robertson, James, *Reform of British Central Government*, London, 1971

Roll, Sir Eric, *A History of Economic Thought*, London, 1953

Rothschild, Lord, *Meditations of a Broomstick*, London, 1977

Rousseau, J. J., *The Social Contract*, and Discourses, trans. with introd. G. D. H. Cole, London, 1913

Runciman, W. G., *Relative Deprivation and Social Justice*, London, 1972

Saunders, John Turk and Henze, Donald F., *The Private Language Problem*, New York, 1967

Scarman, Leslie (Lord Scarman), *English Law—The New Dimension*, London, 1974

Schumacher, E. F., *Small is Beautiful: A Study of Economics as if People Mattered*, London, 1974

Schumpetter, J., *Capitalism, Socialism and Democracy*, 2nd ed., London, 1947

Shonfield, Andrew, *Modern Capitalism*, Oxford, 1969

Smith, Adam, *An Enquiry into the Nature and Causes of the Wealth of Nations*, ed. Campbell, Skinner and Wood, 2 Vols, Oxford, 1976

Strauss, Leo, *Thoughts on Machiavelli*, Washington, 1969

Streissler, Erich (ed), *Roads to Freedom: Essays in Honour of F. A. Von Hayek*, London, 1969

Trilling, Lionel, *Sincerity and Authenticity*, London, 1972

Tuchman, Barbara, *The Proud Tower*, London, 1966

Utley, T. E., *Essays in Conservatism*, London, 1949

Utley, T. E., Review of F. A. Von Hayek in the *Daily Telegraph*, Jan. 10th, 1977

Watkin, David, *Morality and Architecture*, Oxford, 1977

Weiss, John, *Conservatism in Europe 1770–1945: Traditionalism, Reaction, and Counter-Revolution*, London, 1977

Wilensky, Harold L., *The Welfare State and Equality: Structural and Ideological Roots of Public Expenditure*, California, 1975

Williams, Bernard, *The Idea of Equality* in *Philosophy, Politics and Society*, Second Series, ed. P. Laslett and W. G. Runciman, Oxford, 1962

Windlesham, Lord, *Politics in Practice*, London, 1975

Wittgenstein, Ludwig, *Philosophical Investigations*, trans. G. E. M. Anscombe, Oxford, 1963

Index

Advanced Gas-Cooled Reactor, 9

Agriculture, 5; increasing importance of, 17

Alienation, 91, 108

Americium, 22

Amin, General, 23

Anomie, 91

Apaches, The, 106

Aquinas, Thomas, 43

Architecture, damage done by modern fashions in, 117, 142

Aristotle, 43; on property, 49–50, 124

Attlee, Earl, 77

Atomic Energy Authority, 24

Austen, Jane, 41, 109

Bacon, Robert, 76, 135

Baldwin, Stanley, 52, 125–6

Balfour, Arthur, 52

Barber, Anthony, 131

Benn, Anthony Wedgwood, 16, 27, 78, 136

Bentham, Jeremy, 59

Bentink, Lord Henry, 49, 52

Berkeley, Bishop, 42

Bevan, Aneurin, 47

Biffen, John, 63

Bill of Rights, 84–85

Blake, Lord, xi; 51

Bolingbroke, 1st. Viscount, 44

Bonald, Vicomte de, 108

Bright, John, 39, 54

British Empire, economic power of, 38–39

Brittan, Sam, 13, 63, 72

Brown, Lord, 132

Bruce-Gardyne, Jock, 75

Buddha, 43

Bullock, Lord, 19

Bureaucracy, growth of unpopular, 25; lack of theory for management of, 26–28

Caesium–137, 22

Capitalism, Conservatism and, 49–50

Carey, Sir Peter, 27

Carlyle, Thomas, 52

Carr, Lord, 78

Carrington, 6th. Baron, 78

Castle, Barbara, 114

Cecil, Lord Hugh, 44, 52, 57

Centre for Agricultural Strategy, 17

Chamberlain, Joseph, 51

Chatham, 1st. Earl of, 47

Children and Young Persons Act, 1969, 116

Christ, 43

Churchill, Sir Winston, 47, 130

Civil Service, 75–76; limitation on power of, 80–81; and secrecy, 82–83; outsiders brought into, 83–84

Cities, problems of, 18–19, 117, 141–3

Coal Regulation Act, 1842, 54

Cobden, Richard, 39, 54

Coleridge, S. T., 41, 108

Comet, The, 9

Common Agricultural Policy, 17

Commons, House of, reform of, 73–78; and excessive legislation, 114

Community, concept of xii–xiii, 43; account of, 90–96; definition, 92; origins of, 93; importance of stability for, 95–96; and Conservatism, 97–100, 119–21, 125–6; and nationalism, 101–7; industrialism damages, 108–9; inflation fatal to, 109–14; landmarks important to, 117–18

Communism, growth of, importance of in U.K., 36; and Russia, 37; Marx's Manifesto, 56

Co-operatives, 27, 126, 136-7

Compulsory Purchase, 142

Computer industry, British, 9

Conservatism xiii, decline of Conservative growthmanship, 16; account of, 40-46; and the State, 47-50; opposition to laissez-faire, 47; relationship with capitalism, 49-50; and property, 49-50; and historical inevitability, 52-53; and political rhetoric, 68; and incomes policy, 68-72; and need for a philosophy of government, 71-72; allied to Liberalism in seeking constitutional reform, 73-85; and new Bill of Rights, 85; and the concept of community, 97-100, 119-21; relevance to future, 98-100; relevance of, 124-6; principles of, 147-50

Conservative Party, Liberals join, 57; Manifesto 1970, 69-70, 149

Constitutional Reform, 73-85

Corn Laws, repeal of, 48, 51

Corporatism, Corporate Statism, 20, 68-9, 71; account of, 121-3

Crathorne, 1st. Baron, 27

Crichel Down, 27

Crosland, Anthony, 13

Crossman, R. H. S., 82-83

Currency, importance of stability in, 110-11; Roman, 111

Democritus, 54

Deprivation, relative, 16

Deutsch, Karl, 93

Devolution, 103-7

Disraeli, Benjamin, 44, 47, 48, 49, 52

Durkheim, E., 91

Economic growth, impossible to ensure, 13-15; end of, 98; and inflation, 111-14

Economists, dissension among, 14

Electoral Reform, 20, 78-79, 103

Eliot, T. S., 41

Eltis, Walter, 76, 135

Energy, Sources of, 21-24

Engels, Friedrich, 57

Environmental Pollution, Royal Commission on, 22

Europe, Problems of unification of, 28-30

Family, 91

Fascism, 69, 109

Feudalism, 109, 123

Finer, S., 78

Fitzgerald, F. Scott, 101-2

Flowers, Sir Brian, 22

Food, Surplus generated in West, 5

Fox, Charles James, 47

Freud, Clement, 63

Friedman, Milton, 46

Futurology, 3

Gaddafi, Colonel, 23

Galbraith, J. K., xi

General Election of February, 1974, 65-66

Gilmour, Sir Ian, xi

Gladstone, W. E., 47

Gödel, Kurt, 50

Golding, William, 41

Government, growth of, 12ff; secrecy in, 82-83; and inflation, 111-14

Grimond, Jo, 63

Guttman, W., 111

Hailsham, 2nd. Viscount, 45, 58, 84

Harris, Nigel, 122

Harris, Ralph, 63

Hayek, F. A. Von, 46, 61, 62, 71, 80

Healey, Dennis, 131

Heath, Edward, 65, 70

Hecclo, H., 75

Hegel, G. W. F., 49, 56-57

Hirsch, Fred, 16, 40

Historicism, 52-53

Hobbes, Thomas, 41

Honours, Hereditary, 78

Hoyle, Sir Fred, 24

Hume, David, 42

Hutber, Patrick, 63

Immigration, 18

Incomes Policy, 65-72, 130-3

Industrial democracy, Royal Commission on, 19

Industry, shift to populous countries, 5-6; declining industries in U.K., 10-11, 18-19, 134-7; policy proposals for, 134-41

Inflation, 109-14

Institute for Economic Affairs, 63, 67

I.R.A., 106

Isaiah, Book of, 64

Jenkins, Roy, 16
Johnson, Samuel, 42
Joseph, Sir Keith, 16
Jouvenel, Bertrand de, 48, 83, 93

Kahn, Herman, 4, 5
Keynes, J. M., 14, 16, 147–8
Keynesians, 13, 124, 148
Kühn, Thomas, 91

Labour Party, and Trades Unions, 19; decline of, 35–36; 129, 130
Labour theory of value, 55
Lakatos, Imre, 91
Land, distribution of 4; increasing importance for agriculture, 17
Landmarks, importance of, 95–96; destruction of, 117–18
Laski, Harold, 77
Laslett, Peter, 93, 94
Law, Marxist attack on, 56; exhortatory, 66–67
Lawson, Nigel, 75
Leach, Sir Edmund, 91
Legislation, 74–75; effect of excessive, 114–17
Lehrer, Tom, 62
Lenin, V. I., 57, 150
Liberal Party, xi, 57, 63–64, 66, 79
Liberalism, xi; revived, 37–40; and laissez-faire, 47–48; and imperialism, 49; and poverty, 55; account of, 59–72; incompleteness of, 60–62; protection for dissenters, 62; little future for, 64–65; and incomes policy, 65–68; a philosophy for opposition, 71–72; and constitution, 73–85; and new Bill of Rights, 84; and destruction of community, 109, 126; right about incentives, 138–9, 148
Lloyd, Selwyn, 131
Locke, John, 49
Lords, House of, reform of, 76–78
Louis XVI, 47–48
Luther, Martin, 43

Machiavelli, Niccolo, 122
McKenna Tariffs, 138
Macmillan, Harold, 15
Mahomet, 43
Mao Tse-Tung, 46
Marcus Aurelius, 43
Marcuse, Herbert, 59

Market theory, usefulness and limitations of, 39, 64–65
Martin, Sir Leslie, 142
Marx, Karl, relativism of, 41–42, 43, 46; historicism of 52–53; and labour theory of value, 55; and law, 56; and class, 56; flaws in argument of, 56–57; and Communist Manifesto, 56–57, 64; and alienation, 91; and science, 119, 150
Marxism, 43; account of, 51–53, 126, 148
Maudling, Reginald, 16
Meade, James E., 132
Meehan, P., 111
Mill, James, 47
Mill, John Stuart, 61
Mineworkers, National Union of, 65, 68
Mishan, E. J., 98
Monckton, 1st. Viscount, 66, 132
Money supply, 71
Morality, and Conservatism, 43, 147; and Liberalism, 62–63
Morrison, Herbert, 70
Motivation in politics, xii
Müller, Adam, 108

Nagel, Thomas, 62
Nation, definition of, 92; decline of, 99–100; lessening cohesion of, 101–7
National Health Service, 126
Nationalised Industries, 21, 69–70, 130–1
N.E.D.C., 15, 135
Newton, Isaac, 65
Nisbet, Robert, 93
Nozick, Robert, 45, 46, 50, 62
Nuclear power, 21–24
Nuclear terrorism, 23, 99
Nuclear waste, 22, 23

Oakeshott, Michael, 44
O'Brien, Conor Cruise, 104
Oil, British exports of, 9–10; revenues of, 10, 24
Orwell, George, 41

Palmerston, 1st. Viscount, 39
Parliament, accountability to of bureaucracy, 26–27; reform of, 73–83; 'Parliament of Interests', 123

Parmenides, 55
Peel, Sir Robert, 48
Penguin Books, 43
Pevsner, Sir Nikolaus, 142
Pitt, William, the younger, 47
Plant, Raymond, 93
Plato, 54
Plutonium, 22, 23, 99
Population, world, 3, 4; movements of, 4–5; U.K., 140
Powell, Enoch, 38, 52, 53, 63
Press, and secrecy in government, 82–83
Pressure groups, 12
Property, 50, 142

Quesnay, François, 47–48

Racialism, 18
Raison, Timothy, 102
Rawls, John, 62
Referendum, 66; local, 142–3
Regional Policy, 134–7
Retail Prices Index, 110
Ricardo, David, 37, 47, 53, 55, 57, 60
Ridley, Nicholas, 63
Rome, Treaty of, 30
Rothschild, 3rd Baron, 17, 22
Runciman, W. G., 16
Russia, imperialism of, 7; problems of, 7–8; dangers from decline of, 8, 28
Ryle, Sir Martin, 24

Salisbury, 3rd. Marquess of, 52
Scamp, Sir Jack, 132
Scarman, Lord Justice, 84–85
Schumpeter, Joseph, 13
Science, progress in, 91; explanation in, 119
Scotland, 103–6
Scott, Sir Walter, 108
Scottish National Party, 79, 105
Secrecy, in government, 82–83; in local authorities, 143
Sedgemore, Brian, 76
Selden, Arthur, 63
Shaftesbury, 7th. Earl of, 54
Shakespeare, William, 100
Short, Edward (Lord Glenamara), 77
Shortages, 3
Smith, Adam, 37, 47, 59, 60

Smith, Cyril, 63
Social Democracy, decline of, 15, 16, 35–37, 148
Society, definition of, 92
Solzhenitsyn, Alexander, 54
S.S., 106
Stalin, Joseph, 57
State, definition of, 92; role of, 148
Steel, David, 63
Sukarno, President, 114
Syndicalists, 36

Tacitus, 106
Tariffs, 6, 51, 137–8
Taxation, effects of continual changes in, 114–15; need for reduction of, 138–9
Technology, Western lead in, 6; Britain as trader in, 9; and centralisation, 21
Teilhard de Chardin, 53
Ten Hours Act, 1847, 54
Trades Unions, and declining industries, 18; concentration of, 19; new unions, 19–20, 51, 95, 109
Trilling, Lionel, 41
Trotskyites, 36
Tuchman, Barbara, 103

Ulster, 106–7
United Kingdom, problems of, 9ff; devolution within, 103–7
United Nations Charter, 120
Uranium, 23

Vanbrugh, Sir John, 142
Vladivostock, 7

Walpole, Horace, 55
Watkin, David, 142
Weinstock, Sir Arnold, 27
Weiss, John, 108, 122
Wildavsky, A., 75
Wilenski, H. L., 17
Wilson, T., 77
Windlesham, 3rd. Baron, 95
Wittgenstein, Ludwig, 90
Work sharing, 139–41
World Government, 99
Wren, Sir Christopher, 142

Xenophanes, relativism of, 42

TEXAS A&M UNIVERSITY—TEXARKANA